Hughes:
Lion of American Catholicism

Hughes:
Lion of American Catholicism

Richard Daniel McCann

E-BookTime, LLC
Montgomery, Alabama

Hughes: Lion of American Catholicism

Library of Congress Control Number: 2016963115

ISBN: 978-1-60862-674-8

First Edition
Published January 2017
E-BookTime, LLC
6598 Pumpkin Road
Montgomery, AL 36108
www.e-booktime.com

For Finn Thomas, Saoirse Lilliana and Piper Mae

Dedication

This book is dedicated to the Morris County, New Jersey Chapter of the Friendly Sons of Saint Patrick, whose organizational efforts facilitated the creation and design of the Archbishop John J. Hughes Memorial, installed in the courtyard of the Basilica of St. Patrick's Old Cathedral on Mott Street in New York City, and dedicated by His Eminence, Timothy Cardinal Dolan, Archbishop of New York, on Sunday, November 22nd, 2015.

Acknowledgements

This book would not have been possible without the encouragement of my wife, Aine, and the steadfast support of the Morris County, New Jersey Chapter of the Friendly Sons of Saint Patrick, The Bronx, New York and Westchester County Boards of the Ancient Order of Hibernians in America, and Westchester County Division #18, Ancient Order of Hibernians in America.

Foreword

Among the many freedoms long cherished by Americans, and enshrined in the Founding documents of the United States of America, is the free exercise and practice of one's religious beliefs. For one hundred and fifty years prior to the establishment of the American Republic, Dutch, English, French, Spanish and Swedish settlers had established in North America their own enclaves of enterprise and refuge from a Europe they had chosen to leave behind. Some came as freebooters in search of gold; some as indentured servants, and some again as refugees from economic or religious oppression. Whatever their reasons, whether lure of potential riches or the ability to live free of the manacles imposed by the rigid stratification of European society, they came in the hope of eventually carving out a nobler existence, or one at least that would not have been sharply curtailed by an accident of birth. The English settlers differed in that their foray into the American wilderness resulted in the birth of a nation, a nation predicated on revolutionary ideas of life, liberty and the pursuit of happiness. Moreover, it was to be a nation, where the idea of religious tolerance and the free practice thereof, was to be held sacrosanct and enjoyed by all. After a tenuous start in Virginia's malarial swamps at the mouth of the James River, Jamestown became England's first permanent North American settlement in 1607. It was, for that pioneering and courageous group of men and women, a harsh fight for survival. While this humble start marked the beginnings of what was to become a noble experiment, the English colonies possessed different characteristics to the ones established by other European groups. Over the next one hundred and twenty-five years, England solidified

its place in the New World with the establishment of her
thirteen colonies. In these colonial holdings, far from the
English motherland, the philosophical, spiritual and social
underpinnings of what was to become the United States
were born. From its English colonial roots, the new American Republic would inherit traditions of self-government,
independence, self-reliance and freedom to practice religion
in accordance with one's own conscience. In theory, religious
freedom was applicable to all denominations, but as the
basic character of the English colonies remained unalterably
Protestant, "all denominations" was understood to mean
only Protestant denominations.

Ideal fell short of reality, and the notion that America
was a land that championed unqualified religious freedom
from its beginning was a myth. A virulent anti-Catholicism
reigned supreme in most of the thirteen colonies up until the
time of the American Revolution. Catholicism incited the
deepest fears, long held in the Protestant, European memory,
of bloody intrigue and religious warfare. After England
became an apostate nation, as the result of Henry VIII's
disestablishment of Roman Catholicism, it was only natural
that the same prejudices and fears would be transported
across the ocean to England's American colonies. From
interdiction of Catholic religious service to the outright
threat of death to Catholic priests, Roman Catholicism was
repressed and persecuted from the very dawn of its existence in America.

While the Spanish and French who came to North
America indeed had an established Catholic Church and
religion as part of their colonial experience, Catholics of the
English colonies enjoyed no such benefit.

During the worst period of Catholic persecution, (1654-
1763), most of the colonial assemblies passed laws which
forbade Catholics the right to vote or to own land. The
Virginia and Massachusetts Bay colonies, as early as 1642
and 1647 respectively, had enacted decrees that either
proscribed the practice of Catholic religious practice, or
promulgated a death sentence against any clergy associated
with the Pope or the See of Rome. The only significant
exception to this blatant discrimination against Roman

Catholics occurred in Maryland, where Catholic Lord Baltimore, Cecil Calvert, established a colony that guaranteed a
measure of tolerance and freedom of religion for its Catholic
inhabitants, even though the Catholic population of the
colony was a small minority. The fortunes of the colony
turned in 1689, when the Glorious Revolution resulted in
the reinstatement of Protestant supremacy and the installation of William and Mary on the throne of England. These
events triggered a new anti-Catholic revolt in Maryland,
resulting in the defeat and overthrow of the Calvert family.
The American Revolutionary War blunted pervasive anti-
Catholic sentiment, largely because the war forced the colon-
ists to begin viewing the problems facing them from a more
cohesive and "American" standpoint, such as the military
defeat of England, and what form of alliance or government
the colonies would apply to themselves after the English were
gone? From the post-Revolutionary period through the early
decades of the nineteenth century, blatant anti-Catholicism
somewhat subsided. American Catholics, while still very small
in numbers, were learning to survive in a predominantly
Protestant land. Primarily, it was necessary to engage in
accommodation with the more powerful Protestant culture,
which involved both disengagement from doctrinal controversy
capable of igniting friction between the two traditions, and
living quiet, virtuous lives so as to not incur the wrath of
Protestantism in general. This approach was vigorously
supported by the Catholic hierarchy, who literally gave a
pass to discrimination, admonishing Catholics to be prepared to turn the other cheek in the face of attack.

By the 1830s, religious tensions were once again on the
rise throughout the United States, as the result of the
increasing numbers of immigrants entering the country from
lands with substantial Catholic populations like Ireland and
Germany. Sizable numbers of these immigrant groups were
making inroads into burgeoning urban centers like Philadelphia and New York. Catholic immigrants, as long as they
remained relatively small in number, presented no threat to
the existing Anglo-Saxon social order. So long as immigrants
remained within the limits of their own enclaves, they did
not provide the fuel for igniting radical, anti-Catholic

passions. This dynamic changed radically in the decade of the 1840s, when hundreds of thousands of Irish Catholic immigrants, fleeing the horrific effects of famine in Ireland, began flooding into the port cities of the eastern American seaboard. At first the objects of pity, the massive number of destitute Irish began hemorrhaging the established social structure in a way that alarmed the Protestant nativist population. These Irish immigrants were to become the most reviled and unwelcomed newcomers that America had ever received. The hysterical and intensely xenophobic reaction already had precedent in American society, as a nativist mob in Boston had burned an Ursuline convent to the ground in 1834. "No Irish Need Apply" signs appeared in the doorways of businesses and shops, and nativist political parties with names like *The Order of the Star Spangled Banner; The American Protestant Association; The American Party and The Order of United Americans* sprang up to martial the forces of Protestant, nativist antipathy.

When John Hughes left his native Ireland, his dream of becoming a priest had been shelved due to the exigencies of family and economic considerations. This intelligent, square shouldered and somewhat serious young man settled in the area of Chambersburg, Pennsylvania, where a year prior, his father had also come in search of a better material future for the rest of the Hughes family. Eventually, the young Hughes made his way to Mount St. Mary's College and Theological Seminary in the border town of Emmitsburg, Maryland, just a short distance by horseback from Chambersburg. After patiently and persistently attempting to gain admission as a student, fate finally allowed a bright light to illuminate the path for Hughes to continue in his quest to become a priest in the Catholic Church. At an age when many priests were already actively engaged in their religious ministry, Hughes, with Elizabeth Ann Seton's, help, was accepted at the seminary and applied himself with zeal. After his ordination in 1826, he was assigned to the rugged, mountainous area around Bedford, Pennsylvania. It was in Bedford that Hughes came face to face with the pervasive and virulent anti-Catholicism that was so much a part of that era in American history. It was in Bedford that Hughes sharpened his argumentation skills, debating the merits of Catholicism with many of the Lutherans and Calvinists who far outnumbered the small Catholic congregation in Hughes's pastoral care. These same anti-Catholics, who came to respect the young priest, admired his spirit and ability to defend his religious beliefs and his Catholic Church with clear and forceful words. When reassigned to St. Mary's cathedral, the heart of the Philadelphia diocese, Hughes quickly became the favorite of the aging, embattled Irish prelate, Henry Conwell. In addition to applying himself diligently to his priestly duties, he continued to perfect his preaching technique. Memorizing his sermons, he started to gain a reputation amongst not only his congregants, but of the broader Philadelphia diocese as an upright, effective and exceptional young clergyman. In an unprecedented move, he took on in both written as well as oral discussion the eminent Presbyterian, Rev. Dr. John Breckinridge, squarely establishing himself as both an eloquent defender of the Faith and forceful Catholic leader. He was never one to sidestep controversy. Hughes decisively helped in the dismantling of the parish trustee system, whereby pew owning lay persons held deeds to church property and maintained control of priest salaries. For Hughes, only the bishop and parish pastor had the right to govern with respect to "Church" related affairs. A cleric demonstrating talent in the American Catholic Church of the late 1830s was one whose future was bright. John Joseph Hughes was consecrated Coadjutor bishop of the New York Diocese on January 7th, 1838. Ironically, Hughes succeeded the man who had only reluctantly agreed to accept him as a student at Mount St. Mary's, John DuBois.

In 1842, Hughes became the fourth diocesan bishop of New York. It was a unique time in the history of American religion, as the influx of massive numbers of Irish Catholic immigrants fleeing starvation and death altered the nature of not only the Roman Catholic Church, but of Catholicism's place in the United States. John Hughes was the instrument of much of that change. From the earliest days of his priesthood, Hughes became a highly vocal, aggressive and unrelenting defender of his Catholic Church. Whether challenging anti-Catholic slurs made by a Chambersburg, Pennsylvania newspaper, or engaged with anti-Catholic editors like Horace Greeley, Hughes was the first, recognizable bulwark of defense against the common Catholic bashing of the times. With the arrival of huddled masses of his own impoverished, Catholic countrymen, Hughes would spend much of the next two and one half decades both as bishop and archbishop in an unrelenting effort to raise his people up, while simultaneously battling the forces of bigotry keeping them down. While these battles were intense, and waged against nativist politicians, publishers, school officials and common folk alike, Hughes would gain even the grudging respect of his most ardent enemies. Hughes was no glassy-eyed idealist. He explicitly understood that his Irish coreligionists would face many obstacles in their quest to become both assimilated and accepted in a new and hostile land. He knew that this could only become possible by becoming a part of, rather than being a part from. He placed a premium on education, on church building to serve the spiritual needs of the Irish immigrant community, and the regularization of Catholic worship. He extolled the virtues of sobriety, good citizenship, and most importantly, love of America. He ceaselessly worked to show that his people could and would become loyal and true to the United States of America. He condemned secret societies, which he viewed as the residual debilitating effect of centuries of English oppression, and the attempt to expunge the Catholic religion from Ireland. He condemned the revolutionary sentiment that swept Europe in 1848, insisting that the true solution to Irish freedom was not to be found in inadequately supported, short-lived movements bound to fail. He was first and foremost a preacher of Americanism, and oversaw the painfully slow but steady integration of the generation of famine Irish into the religious, social and political mainstream of American life.

Just as any great man, Hughes had great faults. He could be dictatorial and obstinate. His open and oftentimes jubilant nature was capable of coldness and suspicion. He could be unforgiving with respect to slights or perceived injustice, and his ego left little room for the acceptance of competition. He was accused by his most malicious detractors of outright demagoguery, and appeared at times to be indifferent to the needs of the German, French and African-American Catholics also under his episcopal care. He was accused by abolitionists of being a secessionist, as well as pro-slavery. When he reluctantly decided to accept, at the invitation of President Abraham Lincoln, a special mission to appeal to the Catholic monarchial heads of state in Europe for arguing the cause of the Union, he did so out of an unselfish love of his adopted land and its constitution. He was savagely criticized by members of his own clergy for appearing to inject the Catholic Church into the politics of the Civil War. He would never be more roundly criticized than for his perceived lackluster effort in stemming the outbreak of the Irish immigrant led violence connected to the New York Draft Riot in July of 1863. Yet, by the time of his passing in January of 1864, the roots of the Catholic Church in New York and the broader American landscape were firm and unassailable.

No matter how the passage of time may judge John Hughes, there is an inescapable fact: Hughes made possible the emergence of the Roman Catholic Church as the preeminent religious institution of the United States. Catholics of those early years of the American Church could admire Philadelphia's Kendrick for his theological scholarship and Cincinnati's Purcell for his likeable nature and serene demeanor; however, It was Hughes who represented strong and uncompromising leadership in the minds of the Faithful.

Unlike *Bishop John J, Hughes, His Church and the Coming of Age of New York's Catholic Irish*, I have attempted to devote more detailed attention to key events in Hughes's priestly and episcopal career, such as his written and oral discourse with the Rev. Dr. John Breckinridge concerning whether the Catholic or Presbyterian Faiths were inimical to the American way of life; the fight to procure public funding for Catholic Schools, and lastly, his role or lack thereof in quelling the four days of rioting in New York City during the draft in July of 1863. Here again, I am greatly indebted to the work of John Hassard, Father Henry A. Bran and Lawrence Kehoe. I am also greatly indebted to the work of

Rena Mazyck Andrews, Charles R. Morris, Richard Shaw, Monsignor Thomas J. Shelley, William J. Stern, Dr. Patrick McNamara, Robert McNamara and Dr. John T. McGreevy, to name but a few of the numerous scholarly sources used in developing this material.

The appearance of John Joseph Hughes on the American religious scene was destined to prove a key event in the evolution of the American Catholic Church. In the jungle of nineteenth century American religious experience, Hughes's courage and tenacity in the face of attacks against his Church secured for him a place in the pantheon of great Americans. He brought his Catholic religion to its rightful place at the table of the American dream. He may rightfully be viewed as the lion of American Catholicism.

Richard Daniel McCann

Chapter 1

Uneasy Relationship in the Land of Liberty

Most formal histories of American Catholicism begin with the American Revolutionary War, (1775-1783). Catholicism in America long pre-dates this event, and its development is greatly at odds with the often touted but mythical notion of religious freedom. While the early Spanish and French settlers brought their Roman Catholic heritage to the New World, England's claim to territory on the North American Continent resulted in an entirely different history with respect to Catholicism.

It is not surprising that many historical accounts of Catholicism during America's Colonial period barely acknowledge and, even downplay, the blatant, bitter and repressive persecution of the Catholic religion in America.[1] With the establishment of England's first permanent settlement at Jamestown, Virginia in 1607, the fundamental religious flavor of the settlements that evolved into the thirteen "English" colonies turned to Protestantism. The tentacles of anti-Catholicism stretched back to the Protestant Reformation. From this movement, commencing with Luther's ninety-five theses, reform of perceived excesses of the Roman Catholic Church and Papal authority rapidly spread. Luther's translation of the Bible into German both facilitated the familiarity of his own people with Scripture and hastened the development of standard German. In England, the scholar William Tyndale believed that Biblical teachings were greatly at variance with the teachings of Church

1

leaders. His principal contribution was translating the Bible from the Latin of St. Jerome's Vulgate to the English vernacular. Tyndale believed it senseless for a population that only understood English to attend services and participate in religious rituals that were in Latin, a language understood by only a limited number of people.[2] The disestablishment of the Roman Catholic Church by Henry VIII for failure to grant him an annulment from Catherine of Aragon, initiated the English Reformation. This event was followed by the suppression of monasteries, priests and the interdiction of traditional Catholic worship. Polemics such as Foxe's *Book of Martyrs* recalled the torture and burning of Protestants under Queen Elizabeth's Catholic sister, Mary Stuart, who briefly presided over the return of Catholicism to the English realm.[3] France and Spain engaged in a bloody rivalry against Protestant England for the spoils of the New World, as well as abetting English anxieties over attempts to force the apostate nation back into the fold. Catholic Ireland's close proximity to England represented a tempting staging point for the promotion and organization of anti-Protestant intrigue. The second half of the sixteenth century witnessed savage efforts to expunge Catholicism from Ireland.

English Reformation authorities dealt barbarically with the native Irish Catholics, honing skills for administering the same kind of harshness toward Catholics in places like Virginia. A 1642 proscription against Catholics and their priests set the tone for repressive measures to be enacted against the "Popish" church.[4] Add to this the impact of Puritanism, whose zealous adherents populated Massachusetts, Connecticut and Rhode Island. The Puritan world view represented the penultimate hatred of the Catholic Church. The Puritans believed that the post Henry/Elizabethan Anglican Church did not go far enough in purging the tainted practices and beliefs of Roman Catholicism. Starting in 1630, large numbers of Puritans began migrating from England, and within a decade, almost 20,000 had established themselves in Massachusetts and surrounding areas. This migration contributed significantly to the continued disdain of Catholicism permeating early American society.[5]

In the period between 1642 and 1763, laws passed by colonial legislatures reflected a substantial number of prohibitions and impediments against Catholics and the practice of Catholicism. It is important to note that the mistaken notion of freedom to practice one's religion in the thirteen colonies applied only to the various sects of Protestantism. This enshrined concept of American liberty did not apply to Catholics or the practice of their religion.

While Catholics did not live in Massachusetts for at least the first two decades of the colony's existence, it did not prevent the colonial legislature from enacting a law in 1647 stating that any priest, seminarian or missionary ordained by the Pope or by any establishment connected to the See of Rome, would be put to death.[6] Rhode Island, in the first publication of its legal codes in 1719, included an anti-Catholic provision imposing restrictions on Catholic worship and practice.[7] Georgia, the last of the thirteen colonies to be awarded a Royal charter, was proud of its broad guarantee of religious toleration for all except Roman Catholics.[8] Lord Cecil Calvert's colony of Maryland was an exception, as the Religious Toleration Act of 1649 granted religious toleration to all Christians, including the beleaguered Roman Catholic population. This grant was to be short-lived, as England's Glorious Revolution of 1688 resulted in the return to the English throne of the Protestants William and Mary, igniting a new anti-Catholic revolt in Maryland and the removal from power of the Calvert family. The Religious Toleration Act was amended in 1692 and the Church of England became the only recognized religion in the colony.[9] In New York, the fanatical Jacob Leisler wrestled political control from the Catholic governor, Thomas Dongon, spreading sensational rumors that the Catholics of New York were preparing to join together with their French co-religionists and Indians in a Popish plot for the purpose of attacking the English colony. Leisler, declaring himself commander-in-chief, and later lieutenant-governor of the colony, set about removing Catholic office holders and abolishing their right to vote.[10] Pennsylvania's history with respect to Catholics, while progressive, was simultaneously guarded. Of all the English settlements in what was to become the United States,

Pennsylvania's founder, William Penn, was perhaps the most liberal with respect to freedom of religion. In establishing the framework of government in 1701, Penn declared a right of "freedom of conscience" for all persons who believed in God. Though Penn was a sincere advocate of religious freedom, he was concerned about the growth of the Catholic religion. A sad twist in the application of the Religious Toleration Act of 1689 was to have an ironic outcome with respect to Catholics in Pennsylvania. The 1689 Act provided for dissenters from the Anglican religion to have their own places of worship and their own teachers. This did not apply to Catholics, who were believed to be followers of the Roman Pope, and someone that republican minded Protestants considered a foreign ruler. This factor effectively barred any Catholic from holding a public office in Pennsylvania,[11] as no American could simultaneously be loyal to the United States as well as the leader of a foreign power.

The history of anti-Catholicism in the United States was fairly uniform and consistent until the outbreak of the Revolutionary War. Catholics greatly contributed to the war effort against England, and this fact along with the greater developing sense of an "American" identity served to ameliorate religious suspicion and persecution. Other methods utilized by the minority Catholic population against Protestant wrath was to downplay the theological differences separating the two traditions, and not engaging in issues prone to inciting anti-Catholic sentiment. This was to be a characteristic hallmark of Roman Catholicism from the time of American Independence until the middle decades of the nineteenth century.

I

John Carroll, Bishop of Baltimore, and the first Roman Catholic bishop of the United States, was a native-born American and cousin to Charles Carroll, one of the two Catholic signers of American Declaration of Independence. He had been elected a bishop by his clerical brethren in the year of 1789, the same year his friend George Washington was sworn in as the first president of the United States. Typically, bishop appointments were the domain of Rome. Because of critical events taking place with respect to French-Roman Church relations at the start of the French Revolution, Pope Pius VI, preoccupied with these events, allowed the unorthodox manner in which Carroll became a bishop to stand.[12] Carroll was committed heart and soul to showing how Roman Catholicism was compatible with the principles of the new American Republic. Carroll, a strong Federalist and patriot, sought to show how deeply Catholics believed in freedom of religion, even though they had not benefited from the fruits of this seminal American idea. Carroll was a cultured and well respected man. He commissioned the building of a neoclassical style cathedral in Baltimore, and otherwise went about his business as a Catholic gentleman ruling over his small congregation with civility and non-controversy. The same was to be said of his Boston counterpart, Jean Cheverus. Surrounded as he was by the ultra-Protestant, nativist Yankees, Cheverus emerged as a highly regarded churchman of broad-minded, liberal views.[13] In 1820, the Pope appointed John England as Bishop of Charleston, South Carolina. England went even further in attempting to reconcile Catholicism with the workings of the great experiment in American government. In an attempt to show how Catholicism was capable of adapting democracy, he created a written constitution for the Diocese of Charleston, with lay and religious delegates participating in an annual convention. So highly were these innovations esteemed that England was invited to address Congress in 1826. In 1832, the first Roman Catholic priest was named as a chaplain for that body.[14] Attempts at accommodation came with a price. In 1815, the tiny Catholic population of the United States, estimated at 115,000, was scattered over wide and isolated areas, far removed from "organized" churches. To address these deficiencies, priests from the Redemptorist and Jesuit orders went forth along the dirt roads of the American wilderness becoming travelling missionaries. In imitation of their Protestant counterparts, priests oftentimes encouraged their tiny audiences to sing hymns before unleashing fire and brimstone sermons exhorting them to do penance and receive Holy Communion. Like the Protestant Evangelical movement, this kind of Catholic revivalism was well suited to the American frontier. Its emotional nature roused in its listeners feelings akin to a Protestant camp meeting. Revivalist emotion and camp style meetings contrasted sharply with the more serene and cerebral Carroll and Cheverus. One troubling aspect of these mission outreaches was that after the missionary priest left, books would be distributed containing a number of prayers and devotional material, which could be used by any lay person to organize religious activities without a priest presiding. In some areas, Catholics had requested priests and permission to organize parishes. Although obviously not able to say mass, laymen performed other Church services. In many instances, they fully expected to have total say over who would serve as their priest. With respect to Church land, some parishes conformed with the Protestant model of deeding land to trustees rather than to one person such as a bishop or a priest. Catholic bishops decided this was unacceptable, and in their first Council held in 1829, mandated that church property was to be vested solely with the diocesan bishop. The extent to which the early Catholic Church attempted adopting new American methods of governance and administration proved to be the source of great controversy within the Catholic community, not least of which were the problems associated with trustees. Over time, in Buffalo, New Orleans, Philadelphia and New York, conflicts between bishops and boards of lay trustees would become open battle grounds. In Philadelphia, the situation became toxic, when an excommunicated parish priest was supported by the trustees against his bishop.[15]

In spite of attempts to adapt by efforts to democratize, the interlude of peace between Catholics and Protestants was short-lived. After the Revolutionary war, citizens of the infant Republic, engorged on the rational ideas of the Enlightenment, believed their country was pre-ordained to have a special place in the world. The idea of America having a special mission was pregnant with spiritual overtones. This idea infused the national character with an element of perfectionism and unbridled faith in progress. The combination of widespread religious energy and intense social idealism brought about major reforms, advances in human rights, expanded literacy and unparalleled confidence in the future. Even with Enlightenment secularism making deep inroads into American thought, Americans still tenaciously clung to their Protestant religious roots. Fears that secularism was taking root sparked a virulent counter attack, with revivals that soon would grow into the Second Great Awakening. Timothy Dwight, named President of Yale College in 1795, attempted to purify the campus of what he described as a "hotbed of infidelity." Like his grandfather, Jonathan Edwards, the eighteenth century evangelical, who along with George Whitefield ushered in the First Great Awakening, Dwight wanted to use his influence and institution as a spring-board for a rekindling of religious fervor. Dwight started with his Yale students, and ultimately spread out throughout New England. Over the next several decades, not only would Protestant revivals crisscross the county, but the landscape of religious expression would be drastically altered. New sects began emerging and the number of Americans joining Protestant churches in the period between 1800 and 1860 increased six fold. Nothing of the sort could be said of the Catholic Church during this period.[16] Of the 12,860,702 persons living in the United States in 1830, only 5 percent were Catholic. With revivals and renewed Protestant religious fervor, attention once again turned to the "Whore of Babylon", which represented dangers to the high minded republican ideals of America. Perhaps the most potent religious idea distilled from this period was Millennialism. The New Testament Book of Revelation spoke of the thousand year reign of Christ, the defeat of Satan and the final judgement. Among the more prominent teachings of Protestantism was that America, just as ancient Israel, possessed a special place in God's Divine plan. Americans were fulfilling their destinies in a new, untamed and virgin land, perfecting the way to receiving Jesus Christ on the day of his arrival to judge all of mankind. The Catholic Church did not teach a Millennialist doctrine. The Catholic interpretation of the Book of Revelation was viewed in allegorical not literal terms. To Protestants, Christ's defeat of the powers of evil were as real as the sound of blasting trumpets, which would herald the ultimate destruction of sin and death at the end of time. Catholic rejection of the Millennialist doctrine was viewed by Protestants as proof that the Catholic Church did not believe that the United States had a special role to play in the uplifting and salvation of the world. Much of early nineteenth century Protestant synthesis of secular ideas with elements of Protestant religious experience had resulted in the emergence of a society where progress and spirituality became entwined, and ultimately provided the beacon light to a brighter future. This was not the outlook of the Church of Rome, which neither accepted material progress nor the coming of the Millenium.[17]

II

On May 18th, 1844, Professor Samuel F.B. Morse, while seated in a group of hushed and distinguished observers in the chambers of the United States Supreme Court in Washington, D.C., tapped out the first message on his invention constructed of cogs and coiled wires: *WHAT HATH GOD WROUGHT.*[18] The invention of the telegraph marked the start of a revolution in the communications age in the United States, just as innovations in transportation were greatly expanding and facilitating growth of industry and urban areas. Morse, unrepentant in his anti-Catholicism, utilized his revolutionary device to key the following message as well: *FOREIGN CONSPIRACY AGAINST THE LIBERTIES OF THE UNITED STATES.*[19] Once again, Catholicism was under full-blown attack, with vile, anti-papist publications in towns throughout the country sounding the clarion call to stop the advance of Catholicism, and the threat it posed to traditional American culture. In 1834 Boston, an alcohol fueled mob turned its wrath on an Ursuline convent burning it to the ground. The pretext for this violence had been a sermon given by the Reverend Lyman Beecher, a prominent Presbyterian minister largely credited with being one of the driving forces behind the Second Great Awakening. Beecher had preached a sermon about one of his notoriously anti-Catholic writings entitled "A Plea for the West," which roused the listeners to take torch in hand. Violent acts of this nature were directly attributable to the sensationalism surrounding the alleged escape of Rebecca Reed from an Ursuline convent. Reed, a convert to Catholicism, had spent a few months in a religious community. Stories circulated how life within the convent bordered on cruelty. Rebecca Reed allegedly was subjected to daily physical abuse and rarely given food. While neither contention was accurate, a life of consecrated poverty could be austere, but such manner of living in a Catholic religious community was neither new nor unusual. What many hearing these stories failed to understand was that Catholic religious life was influenced by the aesthetic traditions of the "Desert Fathers" and early monastic communities, whose followers sought Christ and a spiritual dimension through solitude and mortification of the bodily senses. Educated Protestants like the Reverend Beecher would certainly have been familiar with religious aestheticism, but it seems that portraying an abused and deprived young girl on the verge of starvation played better to the image of the depravity of a Catholic convent and the broader Catholic Church.[20]

Perhaps the most lurid and incendiary piece of anti-Catholic literature commonly in circulation during this period was a publication known as *Maria Monk's Awful Disclosures*. First published in 1836, nearly 300,000 copies would be sold by the outbreak of the Civil War. Maria had entered the convent and started wearing the black religious habit, as would have been customary for a man or woman entering the novice or beginner period of their religious training; however, on the night of her induction, to her great shock, she found that she, along with several other nuns, were to be used to sexually satisfy the voracious appetites of priests, who supposedly moved with ease through a tunnel that connected the convent with a nearby monastery. With ongoing sexual activity taking place within the confines of the convent, it was alleged that a number of babies were born, baptized and smothered to death by older nuns in the community. Remorseful for having participated in these activities, one of the nuns protested. She was thrown down into a pit with a mattress on top of her, and several nuns proceeded to jump up and down on the mattress until the former had been crushed to death.

The story proved to be a hoax, as Maria Monk's mother confirmed that while she had been in a Catholic orphanage as a child, she had never been a nun and had never joined a convent. She did however become impregnated in Montreal by a vile and profligate former Catholic priest named William Hoyt. Hoyt introduced the Monk girl to a number of gullible Protestant ministers. This group of ministers fabricated the entire Maria Monk lie. William Leete Stone was skeptical. A New York publisher with nativist leanings, he sought permission, while travelling in Canada in 1836, to visit and conduct an investigation into conditions of the Hotel Dieu, the Montreal convent that Maria supposedly had spent her time in. Having obtained permission, he attempted to locate the passageways, caves, tunnels, pits and graves described in the book. Needless to say, they were not to be found. He also conducted a personal interview with Maria Monk, and became convinced that she was a fraud.[21] He accused Maria Monk in his publications of charlatanism, declaring that on the basis of his review of the situation, "I most solemnly believe that the nuns and priests are innocent in this matter."[22] Such statements did not endear Stone to people like the Reverend W.C. Brownlee, editor of *The American Protestant Vindicator* or Samuel B. Smith, editor of a rival nativist Protestant publication with the highly colorful name *The Downfall of Babylon.* Both men had been early and unwavering supporters of the Monk allegations; both men had invested heavily in time and print space to furthering Maria's blasphemous and virtually pornographic description of life in a Catholic convent. While Stone was pilloried for his fair minded pronouncements of the incident, the Maria Monk story gradually started losing credibility and popularity with the general public.

III

American Protestantism was a religion of the printed word. For one to be able to practice the religion, it required the ability to be able to read the Bible. This was the one book that parents on small farms, log cabins and frontier settlements all across America would have had access to, and used to instruct their children by candlelight in the basics of religion and morality. Probably, it would have been a Bible provided by the American Bible Society. Founded in 1816 in New York City by a one-time president of the Continental Congress, Elias Boudinot, the American Bible Society's mission was to spread the word of God, and to end the institution of slavery.[23] In many frontier communities, the Sunday School existed before the common (public) school, and the American Bible Society was in the forefront of building literacy through the learning of Scripture.

The American Bible Society commenced a campaign in 1839 to insure that the Bible was read in every school in the United States. In a largely Protestant nation, there was no disagreement amongst the various Protestant denominations as to the soundness of the proposal. The sentiment was in line with the belief that any education worthy of its name was one which had a Biblical foundation. Horace Mann, generally acknowledged as the father of the public school system in the United States, believed that because the Bible inculcated morality and Christian values, use of it with respect to education was both a necessary as well as invaluable tool in the formation of American citizenry. The one version of the Bible which was looked upon by all the groups within American Protestantism was the King James Version. It was understood that by use of the King James Version, there would be nothing in favor of, or prejudicial against any one particular branch of Protestantism, and therefore was considered non-sectarian. With its universally accepted assumptions of all Protestants, it was the Bible that would be used in public education. The word "sectarian" came to be equated with "Catholic." Catholic children forced to attend the common schools were daily subjected to

Scripture readings from the King James Bible, as well as forced to sing hymns and recite prayers at variance with Catholic beliefs. Anti-Catholic sentiment extended throughout the school program, with pointed reference to deceitful Catholics, vile popery, murderous inquisitions, Church corruption, conniving Jesuits and the Pope as the anti-Christ of the Book of Revelation. In the face of such attacks, Catholics fought back by establishing their own parish schools.

By 1840, approximately 5,000 children attended one of eight such parish schools then in operation in New York City, while an estimated 12,000 more children of Catholic heritage attended no school or were forced to attend the common schools.[24] Schools in America were religious in origin, and retained the religious impulse long after education became a public responsibility. For Protestants, who were raised on "covenant" religion, the Bible served as a blueprint for the training of citizens. In most of the major cities, Protestant foundations supervised curricula, chose textbooks for use in the classroom, and insured that the King James Bible was front and center with respect to the education enterprise. In New York, education was administered by the Public School Society. Its unifying strand was blatant anti-Catholic rhetoric. This sentiment was best illustrated in a New York textbook entitled *The Irish Heart,* which wrote of its fictional hero, Phelim Maghee: "When Phelim had laid up a good stock of sins he now and then... got relaaf by confissing them out o' the way... and sealed up his soul with a wafer, and returned quite invigorated for the perpetration of new offences."[25]

On a March morning in 1859, a ten year old student of the Eliot School in Boston was asked by his teacher to stand and recite the Ten Commandments. This was not an unusual request, for recitation of the Commandments and Scripture Readings was a mandatory practice for school children in the public schools of that era in the State of Massachusetts. The classroom teacher insisted that the reading be taken from the Protestant King James Version. The student to whom the directive was given was one Thomas Whall, a Roman Catholic, who refused to recite the King James

Version of the Ten Commandments. Typically, Catholic students like Whall would have recited a different version of the Commandments, a Catholic version, which would have excluded the Second Commandment recited by Protestants, which cautioned against worship of any "graven image." The entire incident may have passed into history unnoticed had not Thomas Whall declared that his father insisted that he not recite a Protestant version of the Commandments. The refusal of the youngster to abide by his teacher's request touched off a crisis, with meetings taking place between Whall's father, the principal and school committee members to attempt to resolve the issue. The principal was not troubled by the boy's refusal to recite the King James Version; however, a school committee member and one time supporter of Boston's anti-Catholic Know-Nothing Party insisted that the letter of the law be observed. The Whall family were parishioners at the church of St. Mary's in North Boston, and regularly heard sermons whereby the parish priest admonished the people not to allow their children to recite Protestant prayers. The parishioners also passed a series of resolutions, one of which encouraged Catholic children to not be ashamed of their religion. The resolutions also endorsed the practice of students blessing themselves before reciting their own Catholic prayers. A week after refusing to recite the Protestant version of the Ten Commandments, Whall was again asked to recite the same prayers. He refused, and this time he was beaten about the hands by an assistant principal. The half hour beating resulted in severe cuts and bleeding.[26]

While the punishment was being given, classmates of Whall yelled encouragement to him and urged him to not give in. The principal immediately ordered the that all boys not willing to read the Ten Commandments in the King James Version be dismissed from school. In response, about one hundred Catholic schoolboys were discharged. On the following day, the number of students discharged numbered three hundred. The following week, some boys brought in copies of the Catholic version of the Ten Commandments, but once again, they were discharged. Other boys ripped the Protestant Ten Commandments out of their readers.

Assistant principal McLaurin F. Cooke, who had given Whall the beating, was sued by the family for use of excessive force. In a reference to the priest, himself an immigrant, who had told his parishioners to refuse the recitation of Protestant prayers, Cooke's attorney at trial asked "who is this priest who comes here from a foreign land to instruct us on our laws? The real objection here is to the Bible itself, for, while that is read daily in our schools, America can never be Catholic"[27] The court case was decided in favor of Cooke.

The case sparked widespread attention, generating commentary not only in local newspapers but national attention as well. From across the country, young Thomas Whall was hailed as a hero for having stood up to the inhuman torture. He was the recipient of medals and commemoratives from Catholic parishes and schools all throughout the United States, including a goblet from the Cathedral schools of Covington Kentucky.

A number of Boston ministers addressed the topic from their pulpits, condemning Catholic aggression. The Reverend William Buckminster Fuller, pastor of a Unitarian Church near St. Mary's, declared that the "general and common doctrines of Christianity not be banished from the common schools..." An unsuccessful local nativist ticket candidate in 1857, Fuller continued by incorporating other usual anti-Catholic elements into his sermon: "Romanism allies itself with every false and anti-Republican institution which is yet tolerated in our glorious country.... Intemperance and slavery would be quickly overcome if Romanism ceased to exert her influence to uphold them both...."[28] Fuller concluded that should Catholics ever achieve political power in the United States, "our national government, now so fearfully subservient to the shameful slave power, would then be no less under the dominion of priest and friars."[29] Lost in the din of battle was the reality of a ten year old youngster who had gone to school and was beaten for his religious beliefs. In the land of freedom, equality and the supposed enshrined principle of religious toleration, the words inscribed on the goblet given to Whall best characterized the indictment against American Protestantism and the pervasive violence waged against Roman Catholics in the free exercise of their religion: "Filial Piety, manly Fortitude and Heroic Faith Under Torture at the Eliot School, Boston, March 14th, 1859."[30]

IV

The middle decades of the nineteenth century saw the sectional differences between North and South growing more dissonant. The issue of slavery was intensifying these differences, and southern sensibilities with the respect to acknowledgement of slavery as a de facto institution in American society had bitterly propelled itself into national politics. Since 1619, when Dutch traders brought the first African slaves to American shores, the need for human beings to provide the labor needed to work the cotton, rice, indigo and tobacco plantations of the southern colonies had become the support of the South's economy. The South came to be driven by "King Cotton." Southern slavery differed from indentured servitude in that black slaves were without any standing or rights; they were viewed as chattel, property to be bought or sold like animals or furniture. Slaves represented to large plantation holders substantial financial investment. With the increase in the number of black slaves in areas such as Maryland, South Carolina and Georgia, blacks actually outnumbered the white population, and fear of insurrection was always present. As a result, stringent and harsh slave codes reflected the inherent fear whites felt toward the blacks. As a result, slaves were not able to own property, bear arms or leave the plantation without a pass.[31] Aside from the harsh manual labor aspect of slavery, a culture of paternalism evolved around the idea of slaves being protected and cared for by white slave owning masters, which formed the undergirding of a peculiar relationship between whites and blacks in the antebellum South. This paternalistic culture manifested itself in a slave's assisting the lady of the plantation in raising the white children of the household, ultimately becoming a highly trusted servant or even considered part of the family, or of a black male slave elevated to a personal valet or footman for his master, and being taught to read and write. The culture of southern paternalism invariably gave rise to the stereotype of the meek, mindless and content "darky," an innocent child in need of protection. There were some slave owners no doubt concerned about the well-being of their slaves, but many more engaged in physical cruelty, sexual exploitation and rape. Because slaves were viewed as property, they had no recourse in the law, and nothing that any slave-owner was compelled to respect. Racial thinking in nineteenth century America was a compound of prejudice, ignorance, fear and the presupposed inferiority of the African race.

Antislavery sentiment was fed by two distinct intellectual traditions, one from the ideas of the eighteenth century Enlightenment, and from a purely religious standpoint, from the early Quaker pamphleteers John Woolman and Anthony Benezet. To these two men belong the credit for bringing the issue of slavery in the United States before the general public. At the annual meeting of the Society of Friends in 1754, it was decreed that any persons engaged in the buying and selling of human beings was to be expelled. The Quakers enjoyed considerable influence in New England, where in combination with Puritan thought, the forces against chattel slavery gained momentum in the years prior to the American Revolution.[32] The term "abolitionist," and the Abolitionist movement, were the terms used to describe persons in the years before the American Civil War who sought the immediate, unconditional freeing of slaves. Despite the fact Thomas Jefferson was a slaveholder, he had been an advocate for the freeing of slaves, and had even inserted language to this effect as part of the original draft of the Declaration of Independence. The language was subsequently removed by other delegates. Benjamin Franklin had also sought an end to slavery and became a leading member of the *Pennsylvania Society for the Abolition of Slavery*, the first recognized abolitionist organization in the United States. Among Protestant religious groups, the Second Great Awakening inspired a number of social reforms among which abolition assumed the highest priority. For some, this included the immediate abolition of slaves, as it was considered a sin for one human being to hold another in a state of bondage. Abolitionists such as William Lloyd Garrison, Wendell Phillips and Frederick Douglass viewed abolition in precisely those terms, the immediate freeing of all slaves. More moderate abolitionists such as Warren Tappan and Theodore Weld were for abolition, but over a gradual period of time. Some antislavery men like John Quincy Adams did not see slavery specifically as a sin, but rather as a moral defect of society as a whole.[33] During the debates preceding the adoption of the Constitution, the Founding Fathers inherently knew that slavery was a political thorn, and opted to hold the issue in abeyance until 1808. By doing so, it was believed that the institution would end on its own. While illegal importation and trafficking in slaves eventually died away, there were no considerations with respect to what was to happen with the slaves already the property of many southern plantation owners, who would grow more desperately in need of slave labor to sustain the cash crop economy of the South. Neither the Missouri Compromise of 1820, nor the more complex Compromise of 1850 ever held out the prospect of a permanent resolution of the slavery issue, as both proved mere stopgaps in the ever growing bitterness and resentment between the Northern and Southern halves of the country.[34]

For the Catholic Church, the legitimacy of slavery was found in both Scripture as well as centuries of Catholic tradition. Protestant proponents of abolitionism found a ready target for pouring fire at the Catholic position. Archbishop John Carroll of Baltimore had two black servants, one free, one slave. It is estimated that by 1820, the Jesuits had nearly four hundred slaves on their Maryland plantations. Pope Gregory XVI in 1839 issued his bull, *In Supremo Apostolatus,* which condemned slavery as inhuman; however, the wording of the document in several passages left unclear what should happen with respect to existing slaves. There is no question that the document clearly condemned and rejected any new enslavements or any continuation of the slave trade, particularly as it existed in the New World, but examples of imprecise language as seen in the following passage contributed to much controversy:

> "We, by apostolic authority, warn and strongly exhort... that no one in the future dare to bother unjustly, despoil of their possessions, or reduce to slavery Indians, Blacks or other such peoples.... We prohibit and strictly forbid any Ecclesiastic or lay person from presuming to defend as permissible this trade in Blacks under no matter what pretext or excuse, or for publishing or teaching in any manner whatsoever, in public or privately, opinions contrary to what we have set forth in these Apostolic Letters."[35]

Contrary to the British and French empires, where both had declared the emancipation of existing slaves, *In Supremo Apostalatu*s was not, on face, a call to do the same. Historians would debate this point for decades. In any event, to many Catholic bishops in the United States, the ambiguity of the text was interpreted to mean that the owning of slaves was still permissible in the eyes of the Church. The Catholic clergy preached humane treatment of slaves, insisting that blacks, in spite of their servitude, were entitled to the benefits of religious education, unified families, adequate shelter and decent food. Many Catholics viewed abolitionism as a direct challenge to the Constitutional guarantee of a man's right to his property, and the right to have and keep slaves where they already existed. Furthermore, the problem was viewed as one of States Rights, the domain where many believed the issue of slavery properly belonged. On a more practical level, antipathy toward the Abolitionist movement and abolitionists won esteem for the Catholic Church in pro-slavery circles, minimizing nativist opposition to the Catholic Church in the South.[36] America and Catholicism, from the establishment of England's first permanent settlement in 1607 until the middle decades of the 1800s had a relationship vacillating between intense wariness and blatant violence. By the early 1840s, the Catholic Church was still a minority religious sect within the land, its numbers not threatening to the great Protestant majority; its leadership not yet vocal. All of this was about to utterly change, for 3,000 miles across the Atlantic Ocean, events of a cataclysmic social and economic nature were brewing in an island on the fringe of Western Europe. Within a few short years, hundreds of thousands of the poorest and most wretched souls would begin their trek to places like Boston, New York and Philadelphia in leaking, inadequate and overcrowded wooden ships. These desperate migrants would be seeking respite from a raging famine that was to claim one million lives and witness the immigration of that number again. This event was to coincide with the coming of age of a former gardener, who at twenty-six was finally admitted into the seminary to begin studies for the priesthood. This man would have been recognized by others as someone who would have been a success in whatever endeavor he pursued in life, but fate dictated it was to the priesthood he was bound. As fellow Irishmen, the onetime gardener and huddled masses fleeing hunger would be united in America and mutually forge a path leading to a better life both spiritually as well as materially. If ever two more powerful forces were destined to criss-cross at a more critical time, a more needed time, that time had come. Few would say John Joseph Hughes had the most endearing of personalities. What he did have was the fearlessness of a lion, and everything he set out to do for his Church was to serve as a lasting memorial to the power he wielded in his kingdom. By the time his lion's roar ceased, Hughes had secured his Catholic Church, and put his Irish people on the road to political power and influence, not only for the balance of nineteenth century America, but decades beyond.

Chapter 2

An Unlikely Descendant
of the Apostles

In November, 1819, a twenty-one year old immigrant from County Tyrone, Ireland, described by those who knew him as sedate but most respectable looking, was trying unsuccessfully to be admitted as a student to Mount St. Mary's Catholic College and Theological Seminary in Emmitsburg, Maryland. John Hughes, only a few years removed from the harsh experience of being forced to leave his native land, heard that occasionally a poor student would be admitted to the school without pay in exchange for the privilege of teaching and managing students in the lower classes. Hughes epitomized the spirit of the immigrant story in America, embodying a ferocious desire to succeed. Though lacking in formal education, he possessed an acute intelligence, and was pleasing in conversation and manners. He lacked sponsors and proper introductions; however, persistence animated every inch of his being in pursuit of his objective to gain admission to the school. His previous applications had been rejected, but he was never dissuaded from continuing the quest.

The contrast between supplicant and superior could not have been greater. Jean Dubois was born in Paris in 1764, and received his education at Louis Le Grande and the Oration Seminary of St. Magliore. He was classmates with Maximilien de Robespierre and Boston Bishop, John Cheverus. He was ordained to the priesthood in 1787, fled France in disguise at the outbreak of the French Revolution,

21

eventually making his way to Virginia. Letters of introduction and commendation had been provided by the Marquis de Lafayette, and DuBois's initiation into the life of the Virginia aristocracy placed him in contact with the Lees, the Randophs, the Beverlys, James Monroe and Patrick Henry. Elegant, regal and refined in manners, he studied English with the occasional help of Patrick Henry, and while awaiting assignment to a congregation, supported himself by providing lessons in French. For the longest of times, he was the only Catholic priest between Baltimore and the City of St. Louis. No work on behalf of his parishioners seemed too arduous or great, and he was known to travel for days on horseback in the worst of weather to administer the last sacraments to the sick and dying. After fourteen years of tireless pastoral work, he resolved to build an ecclesiastical seminary about two miles from the village of Emmitsburg, Maryland, for preparing intelligent young American men of promise for the Catholic priesthood. The young Hughes was also fond of riding horseback, and periodically would travel the distance from where he lived in the village of Chambersburg to Mount St. Mary's. He was becoming hardened to the usual reply of "no vacancies," but was not discouraged. The word "no" was toughening an already resolute determination to push on. His dedication finally bore fruit. Travelling to Emmitsburg to chance another interview for admission, Hughes stopped at a tavern where he met an Irishman from his home in Tyrone. The fortunate meeting resulted in Hughes being hired to engage in a variety of jobs in and about the Emmitsburg area, jobs that were to put him in contact with respectable Catholic tradesmen, a prominent school master by the name of Mullon, and the parish priest, Father Cooper, whose generosity greatly aided Elizabeth Seton, in the foundation of the Sisters of Charity in the United States.[1]

John Hughes, as he was to prove many times in his life, was not a man to let the will of another stand in his way. By a stroke of good fortune, he obtained work at the convent of the Sisters who ran St. Joseph's school, a short distance from the campus of Mount St. Mary's. Dubois had been a great supporter of the nuns, and the role of Elizabeth Seton was perceived as ancillary to the efforts of Dubois and his clergy assistant, Simon Bruté. An Episcopalian convert, Elizabeth Seton became acquainted with the determined young Irishman. She looked beyond the rough-hewn hands of a laborer, and saw in Hughes the unrepentant spirit of a fighter, not of fists, but of principles. He poured out his tale of rejection. He convinced her that his potential was worth a risk, and in doing so, she sat down and composed a letter to Dubois asking to consider an exception for admitting Hughes. Dubois, while reluctant, could not find it in his nature to refuse a request from such a valiant and vital helper. Dubois determined that Hughes would be useful in filling the role of gardener and overseer for the handful of slaves utilized on the grounds of the seminary. Hughes, in exchange for periodic tutoring, would be given no wages, and provided free board in a log cabin a short distance from the main house. Dubois perceived this was the best arrangement for disposing of the pesky young Celt. It was also a way to acknowledge and fulfill a request made by Seton.[2]

It was at this juncture that the first glimpse of the internal Hughes emerges from the depths of a taciturn and intensive young man, a man who resented having to be the overseer of slaves as part of the condition of his employ-ment. In a stanza from an early poem entitled *The Slave*, the young Hughes, no doubt recalling the slave like conditions of his own native Ireland wrote:

"Hard is the lot of him who is doomed to toil,
Without one slender hope to soothe his pain,
Whose sweat and labor are a master's spoil,
Whose sad reward a master's proud disdain.
Wipe from thy code, Columbia, wipe the stain;
Be free as air, but yet be kind as free,
And chase foul bondage from thy Southern plain;
If such the right of man, by heaven's decree,
O then Africa's sons feel what it is – to be."[3]

Dubois took great pride in his gardens, and often took spade in hand to engage in the physical labor performed by all of the students of the school. John Hughes was supposed to superintend more than work. By the time of his arrival in the early winter of 1819 to take up duties, there was plenty of physical work to be done. Hughes eagerly took up his studies, even though he was not yet a regular student. Over the course of the next year, Hughes would be subject to frequent contact not only with DuBois, but the cleric who was to perhaps have the greatest influence on his priestly vocation, Simon William Gabriel Bruté.

Born of a good family in Rennes, Brittany in 1779, Simon Bruté came of age during the harshest excesses of the French Revolution. Initially a student of medicine, he completed the prescribed course of studies, but opted to follow a calling to the priesthood. Completing his seminary studies at St. Sulpitius, he was ordained in 1808. Two years later he came to the United States with Bishop Flaget, the newly appointed head of the See of Bardstown, Kentucky. It was providential that events brought Bruté to Dubois as an assistant in 1812. Where DuBois lacked sophistication in financial affairs, Bruté compensated with acumen and imagination, resulting in Mount St. Mary's being extricated from numerous financial difficulties. As an academic, Bruté would expand the curriculum and oversee improvement of the quality of instruction. In addition to teaching Latin, French and Natural philosophy, Bruté also acted in the capacity of chaplain to the Sisters of Charity mother-house at nearby St. Joseph's. The Mountain seminary, largely through the extraordinary effort and exceptional energy of DuBois, was now firmly established.[4] Dubois was reluctant to lose both an overseer and someone with knowledge of gardening, so Hughes was often called away from his studies to engage in the type of work for which he had been originally hired. Again, the wheel of fortune turned in favor of Hughes. While pausing for dinner one evening, rather than eating his meal, Hughes was studying his Latin grammar. DuBois happened to come upon Hughes and was greatly impressed by the youth's dedication to study. Dubois decided to put questions to Hughes, and was quickly amazed at how much Latin he had retained in so brief a period of time. DuBois was seeing a very determined man. So much was Dubois impressed by how well Hughes performed, he decided to remove him from a good part of his outdoor duties. It was the first of many milestones for John Hughes, for at the beginning of the 1820 school year, he was finally admitted as a regular student of the college.[5] In allowing Hughes's admission, neither DuBois nor Bruté could have possibly comprehended how great an impact acceding to this request was to be, or exactly how great an influence they were indirectly making on the future of American Catholicism. The American Catholic Church was still a forest in need of trees; the first oak had been planted.

I

The Ireland of John Hughes's birth in 1797 was a land slowly emerging from a century and a half of penal servitude for the Roman Catholic population of the Island. This fate had befallen Irish Catholics in the aftermath of the Treaty of Limerick in 1691, when the Catholic patriots who fought to restore the Stuarts to the throne of England were crushed, and the Protestant ascendancy over a nation whose vast majority was Catholic[6] completed. The establishment of the "anti-popery" and "anti-Catholic" codes were instituted with the intention of eradicating Catholicism for all time. The Penal Laws were designed to preempt Catholics from practicing their faith, hold political office, own land, enter the legal profession, receive an education, live within a corporate town or within five miles of one, own a horse of greater than five pounds value, keep arms, hold a life annuity or rent land valued at more than thirty shillings per year, to name but a few of the proscriptions.[7] The Catholic Church in seventeenth and eighteenth century Ireland had been emasculated. The institutional church was disemboweled. Catholics had no churches, no clergy, and hardly any organization left to speak of. The Sacrifice of the Mass was said in remote areas, mountains, hedges and forlorn places by priests, who were considered fugitives and subject to suffering the penalty of death if caught conducting Catholic worship.[8]

Born in Annaloghan, County Tyrone about one mile from the little market town of Augher on the Blackwater River, the residual effects of the penal period on John Hughes and the stock of Catholic farming people he had descended from was experienced with a greater intensity, as the Ulster plantation under Elizabeth I had savagely uprooted his ancestors to make way for Protestant lowland Scots and Anglican settlers in the late 1500s. John Joseph Hughes was the third child born to Patrick Hughes and Margaret McKenna. Both Patrick and Margaret were similar in that both came from well-respected but not wealthy families. The other Hughes children were Michael, Patrick, Mary, Peter, Ellen and Margaret.

Blessed from birth with a strong constitution, young John Hughes grew with a love for his home and people, sport, hard work and most importantly, a love for the Catholic Faith handed down to him from his mother and father. Patrick Hughes, a modest man in his habits, was upright and better educated compared to many of his peers of the time. He had a love for reading and was a regular practitioner of all things connected to his Catholic religion. He diligently worked to separate himself and his family from the ever present religious strife between Orangemen[10] and Ribbonmen.[11] He acquired a reputation throughout the district as a quiet, industrious, peace-loving man, attributes which seems to have been a factor in saving the life of his son, John. The youngster was caught once by a group of Orangemen, and while pointing the tips of their bayonets at his breast inquired as to who he was. When John said he was a son of Patrick Hughes, the Orangemen released him because they knew of his father and the kind of man he was. A more poignant event, the death of little Mary Hughes, only intensified the resentment felt concerning the prohibitions against Catholics. At the gate of the graveyard, the priest, forbidden entry by law, blessed a handful of dirt before handing it off to a layman to scatter on the coffin as it was lowered into the ground. It was for the Hughes family, especially John, the basis for a bitter resentment that would be carried through life against England and its hateful treatment of the Irish Catholics.

Unlike his father, John Hughes was not destined for a life of farming, for he felt a calling from a relatively young age to the priesthood, and while his parents did not have the resources to finance the needed education for pursuit of such an undertaking, they did encourage to the greatest extent possible the budding vocation of their son. The education for John was largely a local affair, conducted under the auspices of Master Scott, and later on at Auchnacloy near the village of his birth. He received a decent rudimentary English education, but in all likelihood learned nothing of the Greek language and little of Latin. In all his endeavors he seems to have been a favorite of both his school mates and teachers, for his born leadership abilities presented themselves in all activities involving other human beings.[12]

Patrick Hughes, like most of the farmers of his day, gave up a large tract of his farmland to the cultivation of flax, devoting the winter months to the domestic manufacture of linen. While in the neighborhood of Annaloghan, where most of his neighbors were Protestant, Patrick Hughes made the decision to lease another farm in Dernaved. Located about three miles from Annaloghan, the "upper farm" as it was referred to was greatly in need of work, with no immediate pecuniary return in sight; however, this move enabled the Hughes family to be in the company of Catholic neighbors. Over time, a great deal of money was invested into this new farming venture, and when some bad years in the linen trade turned the state of finances at home on the downside, circumstances forced Patrick Hughes to discontinue John's education. Though neighbors were willing to help monetarily in furtherance of the educational aspirations of one who aspired to the priesthood, both Patrick and John Hughes were too proud to consider the acceptance of help of this type. Patrick Hughes was a prouder man, and while his son was forced to return to the work of the family farm, he did not completely put an end to John's love of school or his priestly aspirations. In the same way John Dubois decided that uncultivated talent could not be wasted, Patrick Hughes could not bring himself to totally cut his son off from getting an education, as he believed a decision of that nature would have been a grave injustice to his son.[13]

There was a greater reality for Patrick Hughes to deal with. He was a second class citizen in his own country. Concerned over the decision to remove John from school, he arranged for him to become an assistant to a gardener on a nearby estate, thereby at least trying to keep up the pretense of learning something. It is hard to imagine how young John could have been anything but bitterly disappointed at the whole affair, but nonetheless, obedient to the needs of his family, he continued to work on the family farm. Many people from the Hughes locality were looking westward to America at that particular time, with an eye toward establishing a land claim and livelihood in the fertile farmland of Pennsylvania. Patrick Hughes decided to make an exploratory trip to America, and set out with his second son, Patrick, in search of a new home and life in 1816. The voyage consumed all of his funds, so there was little left to acquire farmland. Upon arriving, he settled in Chambersburg, just a few miles from the Maryland border. While there was no land to be had, there was plenty of work and opportunity beckoned for those willing to put their shoulder to the wheel. Patrick Hughes rented a house and sent for the rest of the family in Ireland. When word reached home, son Michael decided to stay with his mother and sisters because the landlord of the Hughes farm would not extend credit for the crops already growing. Not wanting to lose money, Michael sent his younger brother John.

Accompanied by a neighbor who was immigrating, John Hughes, at age twenty, started on the long ocean trek to a new and unknown world. He would leave Ireland with a burning anger in his heart at having to become an exile. As his journey across the vast Atlantic ocean progressed, he focused on the new country on the other side, a country whose constitution provided that the land belonged to no religion, "a country in which no stigma of inferiority would be impressed on my brow, simply because I professed one creed or another."[14]

II

When John Hughes was removed from his duties in the garden, the school consisted of two log buildings, one in which about sixty boys engaged in academic instruction consisting of Mathematics, English and Latin, and the other where about half a dozen students were studying theology in preparation for the priesthood. Hughes, with virtually little prior exposure to Latin other than what he had managed to master on his own was placed into one of the lower Latin classes. He was still obliged to periodically oversee the garden, which no doubt served as a personal irritant to the studious young man bent on garnishing every hour of study he could. In addition to the garden, he was designated a prefect of one of the study halls. This was not a task that Hughes was enamored of, as the students were prone to making practical jokes with those in authority. Hughes took the pranks in good spirit, and soon the boys realized Hughes was not the best bait for their sense of humor, which included mimicking his Northern Ireland accent. In one instance, a figure representing St. Patrick was hung from the rafters in the study hall, while the unsuspecting Hughes was seated in his prefect's chair at the start of study period. The ring leader of the incident was the son of a prominent judge, and when Hughes caught site of the image of Ireland's patron saint he gazed quietly at the figure and then intensely at the culprit and said, "O tempora, O mores, the son of a judge has become a hangman."[15] Hughes was giving the first evidence of a trait he rigorously cultivated and developed into one his most lethal weapons in the soon to be battles with nativist newspaper publishers and bigots in general, that is, the ability to stand his ground with dignified yet unmistakable and fearless resolve. From an early age, Hughes was already showing that sticks and stones were not going to work. It was also about this time that Hughes started participating in controversies involving any slur or attempt to demean Catholics or Roman Catholicism. Though initially not the best student academically, his work greatly improved upon commencement of his theology courses. In the meanwhile, Hughes continued to perfect his ability to write grammatically correct English, and his seminary peers were soon acknowledging his stature as a gifted and persuasive orator.[16] Writing a reply to a controversial statement against Catholics made at a Fourth of July celebration in the weekly newspaper, *The Franklin Repository,* Hughes vigorously attacked the person who made the remarks. Open anti-Catholic rhetoric was commonplace, so when a friend asked the energetic young seminarian to write a reply, Hughes responded with such acerbity that the editor was initially reluctant to print it. The Catholic hierarchy of the period was loath to exacerbate or fan the flames of Protestant antipathy, so anti-Catholicism in word or action went unchecked and unchallenged. For the sake of peace, Catholics were admonished to live more pious and virtuous lives. In a telling line from a letter written by Hughes to his spiritual advisor, Father Bruté, shortly after *The Franklin Repository* incident, Hughes alluded to the reality of passivity in connection to Catholic religious persecution: "I know that the subject of the controversy would appear too trifling to Mr. Dubois, because he was not interested in it."[17] The controversy of which Hughes was making reference was *The Franklin Repository* article. In marked contrast to DuBois, who preceded Hughes as bishop of the Diocese New York, John Hughes was already staking out a position with respect to his Church, and that position was neither quiescent nor meek. He was already demonstrating the fighting qualities that would later serve him in both moments of great triumph as well as defeat.

In 1823, Hughes commenced his formal theology training under the direction of Fr. Bruté. For his dear parents in Chambersburg, the sight of their son for the first time in his priestly black cassock could have only been equaled by the thrill felt by Hughes himself. It had been a fitting triumph, as the struggle to arrive at this point of his career had been hard fought against the resistance of both people and circumstances. Hughes continued to develop the strongest of attachments to Bruté, the man, who in many ways, Hughes would come to consider the polestar of his priesthood. The same was not to be said of DuBois. To Hughes, Dubois represented one of the major tides of resistance. Hughes never forgot the supplicating involved in attempting to procure placement at Mount St. Mary's. Neither would he forget the casual nature upon which DuBois agreed to utilize his services in the garden as a presumed step to getting a foot in the door toward receiving an education, later described by Hughes as "a regular contract between us, in which neither was required to acknowledge any obligation to the other."[18]

The courage and skill of Hughes as a handler of people was greatly manifested in fighting a fire that broke out in the wooded area around the school. The flames threatened to engulf the small campus, and all of the students were immediately summoned to perform various duties connected to the suppression of the flames. Hughes was selected to act as coordinator-in-chief of the fire forces at hand. He organized fire lines, dispatched persons to specific tasks with respect to fighting the blaze and otherwise assumed full command of the effort. He was an exemplary leader by virtue of his actions, and those around him were obedient to his commands. Having spent an entire night fighting to extinguish the flames, he returned with the best coat he owned nearly burned off his back. He was too poor to buy another one, so he wore the burnt one with a huge patch across the back. Again, in 1824, a fire tore through Mount St. Mary's buildings, burning them to the ground. Hughes, along with his fellow classmates, embarked upon a fund raising project in and around the area to raise the necessary resources to rebuild the structures. In the course of his travels, Hughes began honing his oratorical skills, as a number of anti-Catholic and anti-Papist villagers in and around the Chambersburg area engaged him in debate. Much to the delight of his fellow Catholics, Hughes was mastering the art of presenting logical and persuasive argumentation. He had commenced his formal theological studies at twenty-six, an age when most Catholic priests of the era had already started their ministries. This was not a deterrent for Hughes, whose age and previous life experience was to serve as the sharpener not only of his people and judgement skills, but of his deeper commitment to the religious life he so greatly desired.[19]

John Hughes was ordained to the Diaconate in the year of 1825. He was to be attached to the diocese of Philadelphia, then under the governance of the Irish born prelate from County Armagh, Henry Conwell. When he officially left the seminary, he was to be placed under the direction of Reverend Father Michael J. Hurley, an Augustinian who had gained a widespread reputation as a highly effective preacher. Both Bishop Conwell and Fr. Hurley took a very strong liking to their newest ecclesiastic addition, and Hurley went to great lengths to advise the young Hughes with respect to the multiple aspects of priestly and parish work: "Should you at times find your nerves the least affected by the application of hours, immediately desist, betake yourself to the mountain air and exercise, and beware of enervating in any way that most delicate, and indeed the least understood of the human machine, and which, once relaxed, it is almost impossible to brace up to its original tone."[20] Hurley also advised to have sufficient sermons on hand, "so that when you commence your mission you may be six or seven months in advance of the preaching part of your duty."[21] Invited by Bishop Conwell to accompany him on a diocesan visitation, Hughes, invited to preach at one of the stops by the Bishop, gave what was thought to be a solid performance. Quite unexpectedly, Hughes was asked to preach at a number of other stops. Having failed to take Father Hurley's advice, Hughes gave the same sermon many more times, so much so that Bishop Conwell practically had the sermon committed to memory. It was to be known thereafter as Hughes's "cuckoo sermon."

John Joseph Hughes was ordained on the feast of St. Theresa, October 15th, 1826. At the age of twenty-nine, he had achieved a dream that had first germinated in the fields around his native Annaloghan in County Tyrone, and in the parental love and support of his parents and neighbors. Two weeks after Hughes was ordained, his former superior at Mount St. Mary's, the Rev. Father DuBois, was consecrated Bishop of the New York Diocese. Throughout his journey to reach that most special day in his life, Hughes had demonstrated that he was a man of indomitable will, unbridled energy, courage and a spirit that nothing could break once committed to a course of action. His clerical superiors had early marked out Hughes as one who would go on to achieve great things, and it wasn't long before Hughes established himself as one of the most capable and promising young clergymen of the Philadelphia Diocese. First assigned to the rugged, mountainous area around Bedford, Pennsylvania, an area populated by anti-Catholic Lutheran, Calvinistic and Wesleyan immigrants, Hughes immediately threw his spirit into debate with the detractors of Catholicism, eventually winning over some of the strongly antagonistic Protestant elements in the area. He gained both respect and even friendship of many of these Protestants through his resolute and unyielding defense of his Faith. Even the greatest of these Catholic detractors found something admirable in the "pluck" of this audacious young priest.[22]

This was the molding time for Hughes, for he was now coming face to face with aggressive and pervasive anti-Catholicism in his day to day work. These experiences were to further hone and shape the future arguments of a man committed to the destruction of bigotry, experiences that could not be learned in the theology textbooks of the seminary. Though his greatest battles against Catholic prejudice were still more than a decade and a half in the future, the clear outline of a mental, two-fisted brawler was fast emerging. In a segment taken from one of his early poems penned in 1825, "*Ode to Death,*" Hughes gives an indication of his fondness for striking blows against every sort of falsehood:

> "King conquers king, and slave his fellow-slave;
> But slave and king shall fall
> In thy sepulchral hall;
> Whilst thou, grim monarch, shall triumphant wave
> Thy iron scepter o'er their equal grave,
> Dread conqueror of all!

Those fools who fight for lords and thrones,
To thee at length shall yield,
The helmet, lance and shield.
When princely pride shall ask their dying groans,
Or wish the tribute of their valiant bones,
To whiten on a field.

Yet be not proud in thy restless sway
Thou scourge of human crime
In every land and clime;
For on the confines of eternal day
Thou shalt fall, an angel's easy prey,
Upon the tomb of Time."[23]

The aged Bishop Conwell was extremely enthusiastic about Hughes, and the fact that he had preached the same sermon several times as a deacon did not deter Conwell from according accolades on this young cleric of promise: "Ah, Hughes is the boy isn't he. He takes all of the wind out of our sails. We'll make him a bishop someday."[24]

In Conwell's diocese of Philadelphia, a diocese rife with dissent and full of problem priests, the decision to recall Hughes from Bedford in 1827 was viewed as a needed potion, for Hughes was already demonstrating a trait that would remain constant throughout his career... strict obedience to the Church's chain of command. Because of this, Hughes became Conwell's "young man."

There was no question that from the start, John Hughes was perceived as a man loath to serve any but his legitimate masters; he belonged totally to the Church. His natural born fighting instinct however seemed to harbor trepidation with respect to the tumultuous state of affairs of the Catholic Church in the "City of Brotherly Love," for the Church seemed neither brotherly nor in any way committed to the Christian message of love. The idyllic community of Mount St. Mary's had made a profound impression on Hughes, and the setting and personages who engaged him both in his academic studies and development of a spiritual life appealed more to his introverted nature. There was a huge difference in the rural, somewhat secluded life of Bedford and Mount St. Mary's compared to the cloak and dagger intrigue of urban clerical politics. It was at this juncture that Hughes quietly considered leaving the diocesan priesthood and applying to become a member of the Augustinian order. Whoever counseled Hughes on the matter, the thought of leaving the diocesan priesthood was dropped, and Hughes returned in late 1826 to the Mount to prepare for his departure for Philadelphia. With $3.50 in his pocket, Hughes left Emmitsburg forever. Hughes was accompanied in the stage coach by the newly consecrated Bishop Dubois, unknowingly making his way to a different kind of hell on earth in New York. The meeting of the two under these circumstances proved ironic, for in the message sent by Dubois offering Hughes congratulations on his ordination, he wrote, "my ever dear child and reverend friend," hoping that "we may reunite one day where we can no more be separated."[25]

Chapter 3

Lessons in the Rough and Tumble of Diocesan Life

By 1820, the City of Philadelphia had been without a bishop since the death of its first, Michael Egan, in 1814. In the six years that the See had been left vacant, prominent laymen became increasingly jealous of who was to have a say in the hiring and firing of the priests periodically turning up in the diocese. It was around this time that Father William Hogan, suspended from the priesthood in Dublin, turned up in New York to offer his services in furtherance of the Kingdom of God. Accepted by New York's Bishop John Connolly, Hogan was sent to the far off reaches of Lansingburgh, New York, about as far removed from civilization as one could be, even by the standards of 1820. Having conveniently forgotten to reveal his suspension, the young Irishman was virtually like a newly minted coin; he had no past as far as the American Catholic Church was concerned. He also realized that his priestly ministry need not be limited to such a crude backwater as Lansingburgh. In the spring of 1820, Hogan struck out for Philadelphia, and found priestly work after managing to favorably impress the trustees of St. Mary's parish. St. Mary's was a neat red brick building located across the street from Independence Hall, a far cry from the upper reaches of the Hudson River in New York. Hogan, with his boyish good looks, flamboyant style and better than average preaching abilities, impressed his new congregants. He was different from any previous cleric who had served at St. Mary's, and went beyond the normal stations of a

37

Catholic parish priest, eventually installing himself as part of Philadelphia society.[1]

While these events were taking place, Rome needed to fill the vacant See of Armagh in Ireland. In tradition, this was the See of St. Patrick, and the candidate in line for receipt of this episcopal chair was seventy-three year old Henry Conwell, who had been Vicar General for over a quarter of a century. Because of the delicate situation with respect to the English government and the virtual slave status of Roman Catholics in Ireland, a tactful appointee was needed to fill the position, and Henry Conwell, in the eyes of his brother bishops, was not the man who fit the bill. In order to remove Conwell from succession to the See of Armagh, it was decided to appoint him Bishop of Philadelphia. Upon arrival, Conwell immediately ordered Hogan to assume the life style of a priest. Hogan refused, and from his own pulpit declared that nobody, not even a bishop, had the right to tell him where and how he was to live. In response, Conwell declared that Hogan was suspended; the elderly prelate was about to be taught a lesson in American democracy.

The stage was now set for a confrontation with respect to control of the assets and personnel of the Catholic Church in Philadelphia. This confrontation was to affect not only the diocese of Philadelphia but the broader Catholic Church in America. It was also to profoundly impress a young, newly ordained cleric named John Hughes, whose involvement in the unfolding conflict would create in him a mindset that was determined to retain the unequivocal control of the Church in the hands of clergy. Never again would the laity dictate what priests were retained, what they were paid, where and how they were to live, and most importantly, interfere with a bishop in the administration of his diocese.

The root of the problem lay in the system known as "Trusteeism." The system grew out of the early American Catholic Church's practice of allowing the pew holders, who purchased their own seating in the church, to have a say in the administration of parish affairs. Laymen were elected by the pew holders to act as trustees, whose function, in theory, was to advise and assist the parish priest in managing the non-spiritual aspects of day to day parish activities. On the positive side, congregants providing a financial investment would presumably have a greater stake in the well-being of their church. Over time, the trustee system inevitably led to bitter conflicts within churches, with one group of trustees fighting to gain control over another. Parishes became highly factious, often turning into bitter political battlegrounds. Perhaps the worst aspect involved cases where unscrupulous individuals gained control over church property, priest salaries and even clerical appoint-ments.[2] In Conwell's way of thinking, his ordering Hogan to cease and desist in the undignified manner in which he was carrying on was within his absolute right to do as bishop. In the same manner, his suspending of Hogan from ministry was just the next logical step for his refusal to obey a direct order. The trustees and a number of the congregants of St. Mary's took Hogan's side in the controversy. Further compli-cating the situation was the charter under which St. Mary's had been organized. The charter of the church stipulated that the property was to be vested in a board of trustees consisting of the pastors, not numbering more than three, and eight laymen all to be elected by the pew holders.

The bishop claimed sole right to appoint and remove and the lay trustees made it clear they were as determined to do the same. The trustees proceeded to make Hogan the pastor and to take forcible control of the church. In the face of this defiance, the aged Conwell moved himself, the other clergy in his household and a sizable number of congregants to the chapel of St. Joseph's, a short distance from St. Mary's. After Conwell's departure, Hogan had a number of new pews built in the church and put in one hundred thirty new voters of his own faction, many of whom were avowed enemies of the Catholic Church. In the next election of trustees during Easter week of 1822, the Hogan faction retained control by a slim majority, but the event was marred by bloodshed and violence. Charleston's Bishop England attempted to reconcile the parties, but was impeded from accomplishing this task due to Hogan's lying and insincerity. The problem took a bizarre turn for the worst, when Bishop Conwell sent an invitation to Father Vincent Harold. At the time, Harold was prior of the Dominican convent in Corpo Santo in Lisbon, Portugal. Harold had a reputation for being an eloquent and popular preacher. He had also spent some years in Philadelphia. The plan was to have Harold win over the malcontents of St. Mary's, enticing them away from their disdainful pastor and leaving him without a congregation. The invitation had barely gone out when Conwell learned that the very same priest he was summoning to save the church was the principal leader supported by the trustees of St. Mary's in the same type of situation against Bishop Egan. Conwell was apoplectic, and immediately revoked the invitation; it was too late! Harold arrived in Philadelphia to take up his new position in December of 1822. Initially, Harold was appointed Conwell's secretary. At first, he took on the dissidents with great energy. The efforts to weaken them proved unsuccessful. Hogan was eventually condemned by the Holy See, but this too was unheeded. In 1824, Hogan left the parish of his own accord, turned Protestant and married. The apostate priest started writing books and pamphlets of a violent, anti-Catholic nature, often featuring extreme criticism of Conwell, England and the Philadelphia clergy. Shortly afterwards, another Irishman, Thaddeus O'Malley, arrived to take up the pastoral duties vacated by Hogan. Bishop Conwell offered terms of accommodation, but these were rejected, and O'Malley set out for Rome to lay the complaints of the trustees of St. Mary's before the Pope, as well as request removal of the Bishop. So intense had the feud at St. Mary's been that children in their games divided themselves along faction lines, one in support of the Bishop, the other in support of the trustees, these no doubt inspired by the divisions of their parents. The intense feelings generated over this conflict would be felt long after the events had finally come to rest. Conwell was an amiable man, but unfit for his post. He understood little of the conditions of the American Church, and advancing age and the stress of the entire affair at times seemed to render him totally incapable of clear thought or constructive action. On the brink of being completely worn out, Conwell made another regretful decision on October 9th, 1926, by signing a treaty with the trustees, a treaty that sacrificed certain fundamental principles of church government. A temporary peace followed the signing, but the treaty itself was certainly not one that would be accepted by the Holy See. Basically, the document called for the bishop to be recognized as the senior pastor, who was to retain the right of appointing two assistants. If the trustees did not agree with the appointments, they were to state their objections, and if the bishop still persisted with respect to the appointments, he, along with two clergyman not connected to St. Mary's, were to meet with three of the trustees, and a majority vote within this group would settle the dispute. In the event of a tie, the parties would select an individual who cast a deciding vote. The salary of the clergy and bishops was left to the discretion of the trustees. Additionally, all deeds, papers, documents and books belonging to the corporation were to be turned over to the trustees.[3] Peace was restored, the interdict against St. Mary's was lifted and Fathers Harold and Heyden were appointed pastors. The treaty was sent to Rome for the review and approval of the Pope, but all but the most misinformed enthusiasts knew that such a treaty would not survive and would be annulled. Conwell had effectively abdicated his role as bishop, and the trustees did little to mask their jubilation and contempt for the old man. Again, the interval of peace was to be a short one.

I

It was Father Heyden who urged the bishop to bring John Hughes into the cauldron that was the diocese of Philadelphia proper. While on mission in Bedford, Hughes had lived with Father Heyden's parents, and having developed a lasting attachment to the family, wrote to Heyden's father that "you will not be surprised at receiving a few lines from one who spent a brief but happy time under your hospitable roof. The recollection of that short mission, when to me everything was new, only fills me with regret that it terminated so soon, whilst at the same time it reminds me of the many obligations I owe to your kindness and to that of your amiable family."[4] Heyden was anxious to return to his previous country assignment around Bedford, and he hoped that Hughes would replace him. On the contrary, Heyden was kept at St. Mary's, and Hughes was assigned to St. Joseph's, which Conwell had hoped to eventually make into a separate parish. It would have been an overwhelming situation for any new man, but Hughes held his tongue and avoided conflict as much as possible. It was not that he was afraid to come out openly against the enemy, for his fighting nature was primed for battle. Hughes's loyalties were unquestionably on the side of his elderly episcopal countryman, and in following the church's chain of command. This was a delicate situation, for Hughes now had to learn to deal with a more subtle kind of enemy, an enemy who came disguised as a friend. He was fortunate in that early in his priesthood he had received prudent counsel by Fathers Hurley, Heyden and Bruté. The experience of these men would help the young Hughes navigate the first steps in the minefield. Writing to Hughes shortly after the notice of being reassigned from Bedford, Hughes received from Father Michael de Burgo Egan, successor to John DuBois at Mount St. Mary's, a letter of consolation and encouragement. Egan, though sorry on the one hand to see this young priest of promise cast down into so pitiful a place as metropolitan Philadelphia, utilized the opportunity to remind Hughes of his own personal character and strengths, and of the great contribution he could exert on behalf of the Faithful.... "It is but a few days ago that I learned you had been recalled from Bedford and stationed in the miserable city of Philadelphia. I was surprised to hear it, and from my soul I pity you, for I have some idea of Philadelphia. But as it is evidently the will of God that called you, or rather which you obeyed, you have not so much to fear as in place of your own choice. You have a vast field before you, in which you can exert your zeal and labor for the glory of our common Beloved. I feel deeply for the state of the Church in Philadelphia, and am convinced that it has need of zealous, disinterested and holy priests to keep alive the spark of religion which still exists in the breasts of a few."[5] Hughes was biding his time. He would make no pronouncements with regard to the still simmering difficulties at St. Mary's until the verdict of the Holy See had been returned. He would never discuss his feelings about Church authority to any but those who were his closest confidants. Though there were other eminent Catholic preachers, the sermons of John Hughes began to take on the characteristics of his later discourses. He prepared them meticulously, memorizing them by heart. He was making an impression on the public and his bishop was elated at seeing the emergence of such a promising career. The advice given to Hughes from all quarters was sound, for clerics like Father Bruté firmly believed that once the articles of the peace treaty signed by Conwell became known in Rome, the fallout would not be pleasant. The old bishop had directed his vessel into the eye of a hurricane, and Bruté felt that anyone associated with this insanity would be irrevocably hurt as a result. Father Michael Egan cautioned Hughes "to keep on the best side and most friendly terms with Father Harold, and convince him that you never meddle or intrigue in any way."[6] Conwell had grown even more intractable than before, and asserted that because of the insulting and vile manner in which Harold had spoken to him and about him, there was no possibility of appointing Harold as Vicar General of the diocese. Harold demanded specifics with respect to the charges leveled against him and the battling at St. Mary's began once again. This time Conwell decided to move against Harold by suspending him and by having all of the priests of the diocese sign a document stating to the effect that the bishop had not acted in an uncanonical manner by ordering such suspension. Hughes was in a quandary. As one of the newest priests, he did not want to be forced to sign anything or do anything as if to implicate him in events he had no real involvement in. As a matter of obedience, Hughes was prepared to sign if told to do so. When commanded by the bishop to attend a clergy meeting and advised that the document he would be signing would never see the light of day, Hughes relented and signed. What happened next was to prove a disaster for Harold and his trustee faction, and a great victory for Hughes. When advised of the suspension order, Harold calmly accepted his fate but did so with a sinister motive. Harold played the insipid articles of peace sent by Conwell to the Congregation of Propaganda[7] as a means to become bishop of Philadelphia. Harold believed that once the Vatican realized that the doddering octogenarian Conwell would ultimately be viewed as the source of all the trouble, he would be retired and removed.

Harold was banking on being viewed as a man of ability, popularity and the strongest of possible replacements for bishop. At this juncture of the intrigue, Harold made a serious tactical blunder. When word of the suspension started to become known by the general public, Harold felt the necessity to vindicate his reputation with the good Catholics of the city by suing for defamation of character. Desiring to make an example, he chose the least experienced, least involved and potentially most vulnerable priest for having signed the documents authorizing the suspension: John Hughes. The desired effect had been achieved. Hughes was now cast as a villain equal to any who had preceded him. Hughes, as a priest of growing stature in St. Joseph's, was now put into an impossible situation. Conwell demanded he come around the corner to St. Mary's to act as pastor in place of the suspended Harold. It was not a good situation, and Hughes's mentors and friends urged him to stave off this request for as long as it was possible. With no recourse, Hughes took up his position in the very heart of a warring parish. The congregants were not happy and because both Hughes and his assistant, Father Reilly, had been appointed by the bishop and not formally hired by the trustees, neither Hughes nor Reilly were given a salary.[8] Hughes masked his real feelings about the desperate situation he now found himself in. Writing to Bruté, Hughes with intense frustration asked: "What will become of the Church if laymen, sometimes as depraved as they are ignorant, have such influence in her government? What will become of the clergy, if they must descend from their sacred character, and become parties and tools of parties in the petty broils of contending rivals for the office of trustee? And for what advantage? Just to have the choosing of their masters? There is no remedy for all of this until the time shall come to aim the blow, not at the branches, but at the root of this abominable system of trusteeing churches."9 In spite of his troubles, Hughes continued to perform his duties with enthusiasm and discretion. He refused to discuss any of the troubles with laymen. While he found it all a debasing and disheartening experience, he did not give into the impulse of whining self-recriminations, which would have been the hallmark of a lesser man. To Hughes, the Church was not a game of politics to be bartered and compromised in some back room. Suddenly, the awkwardness of the situation forced out of him the greatness that was to become a part of the Hughes trademark. He perfected his sermons, and with a growing self-confidence, John Hughes the pastor was starting to assume a position more comfortable with being an authoritative figure rather than a meek and retiring junior priest. The people of St. Mary's started to notice his forceful, intelligent and attractive characteristics. Hughes was growing in stature and popularity with the quarrelsome congregants of the Cathedral Church of Philadelphia. Some of them even felt comfortable in knowing that should the Vatican return a negative verdict with respect to the terms of the treaty, they would not in any way be ashamed that such a person as Hughes was now leading the parish. As the popularity of Hughes continued to grow, Harold began to soft pedal the lawsuit. The affair was ultimately dropped. Harold was starting to regard Hughes in more circumspect terms, believing it better to have Hughes as a friend rather than a foe, especially if his plan of attaining the Philadelphia episcopacy became a reality.

Hughes and Reilly were still without salaries, and the trustees decided to hold that situation in abeyance until there was a final verdict with respect to the principle issues at stake. Hughes was now ready to turn the tables on St. Mary's, a parish that always regarded itself as the crown jewel of the diocese. Refusing to wait for word from Rome, Hughes, aware that the real issue was if whether St. Mary's believed any priest was worthy enough to serve the parish, startled his parishioners at Mass one Sunday by stating that as the people at St. Mary's didn't seem interested in assuming their obligations and responsibilities, he was no longer interested in being their pastor. Resigning, he took his assistant, Father Reilly, and returned to St. Joseph's. St. Mary's was now without priests. Harold had been out-smarted, as he could not very well move into fill the vacuum for fear of losing the moral posture he so desperately wanted the Vatican to see. Old Conwell inserted the stinger even deeper by offering to say a Mass for St. Mary's each Sunday morning at 9:00 A.M. It was for John Hughes a singular triumph, one which not only increased the genuinely deep affection that Conwell felt toward him, but a wary public as well. This was the John Hughes that parishioners for the first time were coming to understand stood head and shoulders above the venal and low caliber clergy they were used to dealing with. In the spring of 1827, the verdict predicted by both Fathers Egan and Bruté had finally made its way back across the Atlantic divide. The Vatican roundly condemned the compromise agreement that Bishop Conwell made with the trustees as it was calculated to "overthrow the episcopal power."[10] The condemnation was promulgated throughout the Philadelphia diocese, and Conwell was sum-moned to Rome, compliments of the Pope. In the aftermath of the promulgation, Reverend Father William Matthews of Washington was appointed administrator of the diocese. Harold and his underling, John Ryan, both guilty of having committed numerous acts of insubordination, received from the Congregation of Propaganda and the Vicar-General of the Dominican Order notice to immediately vacate Philadel-phia and proceed to Cincinnati. Hughes was already being considered for the bishopric of that See, largely on the strength of Conwell's bombarding Rome with the assertion that Hughes should be made a bishop at the earliest, possible time. Hughes, writing to his dear mentor Bruté on May 14th, 1828, reflected with a tone of pity on the final outcome of the Philadelphia debacle: "I will offer no com-mentary. Perhaps we will all be in the grave before Divine Providence shall have manifested its mysterious designs by drawing great and lasting good from transient evil. The shepherd has been stricken because the flock was divided, whereas there ought to have been one shepherd and one sheep-fold. They have all *preached* obedience to lawful authority, but now it is in their power to *preach effectually*, by the practice of their own doctrine. I hope they will."[11] The bizarre flame of this tragic episode in American Catholicism had not yet been fully extinguished. After Conwell set out for Rome, Harold appealed to Secretary of State Henry Clay, seeking a mandate of protection from the democratic government of the United States of America against the tyrannical mandate of the Roman Pope. It was a mystery as to how Clay was expected to formulate a position as Secretary of State that would absolve the two errant priests from upholding their vow of obedience?

Even President John Quincy Adams, no lover of the Roman Catholic religion, felt empathy for the two priests. Ironically, Father Ryan had never become a citizen, and he throttled himself into high gear to become naturalized in order to gain the protection afforded by the democratic institutions of the United States. The political appeal to the civil government disgusted Hughes, who caustically commented that "Hogan talked about it, but they have done it."[12] As there was no American representative to the Court of Rome, President Adams directed that the United States Minister to France, James Brown, raise the matter with the Papal Nuncio, Monsignor Luigi Lambrusschini. Their meeting in September of 1828 was unique in that the diplomatic representative of the young American Republic was sitting down to discuss with the spiritual representative of the Catholic Church, long held in villainy by both Protestant Europe and now the United States, an issue concerning religious freedom. While Brown assured the Nuncio that it had no interest in interfering in the spiritual aspects of the problem connected to Harold and Ryan, it did feel compelled to provide temporal protection for two of its citizens. Monsignor Lambruschini basically informed Brown that neither man would be interfered with, and that the demand for them to leave Philadelphia to go to Cincinnati was in keeping with the vow of obedience, which both men had pronounced as part of their religious life. In support of that claim, Monsignor further pointed out that in the spirit of such obedience, the Bishop of Philadelphia had voluntarily left for Rome upon request from the Pope, where neither of the two men in question would abide by such a request. Brown, somewhat brushing this fact aside, continued to press the case with respect to recognition and maintenance of the democratic rights of Harold and Ryan. President Adams respected Harold, as both were educated men of literature. The real issue finally emerged. If it was believed that Catholicism was a threat to American liberty, events might someday result in the United States denying the Catholic Church the right to freely exercise its rights and prerogatives within its own ecclesiastical jurisdictions. With this in mind, Lambruschini quickly assured Brown that the Church had no civil authority whatsoever over Harold and Ryan. He stated that they had both taken vows, one of which was a vow of obedience. If both men no longer wished to abide by the rules of the Church, they were free to walk away from the vows they had taken. In the absence of doing that, they were required to follow the rules and laws of the Church in the same way that an American worker, not satisfied with the way a shop was being run was free to leave it, otherwise, he was bound to accept and to discharge all of the rules and laws associated with same. In the end, Secretary Clay, having reviewed the results of the meeting as well as receiving letters from the Archbishop of Baltimore and Father Matthews further supporting the contentions of the Nuncio, determined the matter to be strictly spiritual in nature and was dropped as far as the United States government was concerned. Both Harold and Ryan continued their rantings about the matter for almost another year. Shunned by their brother priests, they had run out of options.

Finally, both men returned to Ireland, spending much of their remaining priestly years castigating the American Catholic Church, particularly, the Philadelphia clergy.[13] Hughes, returning to St. Joseph's in the aftermath of the turmoil involving the St. Mary's trustees, continued growing in stature with his flock. He was instrumental in the establishment of an orphanage for the care of destitute Irish children, bringing the Sisters of Charity from Emmitsburg to assist in this work. It was also the time that Hughes commenced in a formal way to answer attacks against the Catholic religion. Hughes believed that too much energy was being expended on battling the petty and venal forces within the Church as opposed to battling the real enemies that stood at the gate. It was an age of anti-Catholicism and Philadelphia, just as other parts of the country, was not without its anti-Catholic bigots.

II

As a young man, Hughes had suffered under the cruel penal laws that had been imposed on the Catholic population of Ireland. When Catholic Emancipation was achieved in 1829, Catholics were once again able to participate in areas where they had been previously barred. George IV gave his assent to the Emancipation Bill on April 13th, and as soon as word reached America, a Mass of Thanksgiving was celebrated at St. Augustine's Church on May 31st. The homily was preached by Hughes, who dedicated it to Daniel O'Connell. His mighty efforts were the singular, greatest force in overcoming the evil, immoral and servile state under which the Roman Catholic majority was forced to exist for 150 years.[14] Hughes, who had known the lash of the penal laws as a child in Tyrone, proclaimed to the packed congregation with a great sense of personal satisfaction that "it was an occasion of legitimate rejoicing in every sense: when the apple of discord, which has been the cause of so much oppression, injustice and bloodshed in unhappy Ireland, has been at length destroyed, and the axe effectually applied to the root of the tree that caused it – when these inequalities in the law which divided the nation so long, operating as almost an irresistible incentive to the worst passions of authority, are blotted out forever – when we hope that hereafter will be more outraged by the crimes of the oppressor; that humanity will no longer be compelled to weep over the sufferings of the oppressed – when in fine, the kindred virtues have been permitted to meet again, and justice and peace have actually kissed, in token of eternal amity."[15] Not everyone shared the jubilation accompanying the reality of Catholic Emancipation. The *Church Register,* an organ of the Philadelphia Episcopalian Church, edited by the reverend W.H. DeLancey, D.D., used the occasion to attack both the Catholic Church and the Irish. In a series of articles, DeLancey expressed fears and reservations concerning the restoration of full citizenship status to the Irish Catholics in the British Empire. The *Register* opined on the dangers of according the new freedoms to a "superstitious and corrupt church."[16] Continuing the onslaught, it noted: "We shall be sorry for the measure if the revival and dissemination of the trumperies and delusions of Popery are to be the result of it."[17] In response to these attacks, Hughes fired off numerous replies in the *United States Gazette*, and for the first time started to sign his name to the pieces he submitted. In response to Hughes, the Reverend DeLancey stated that it was not the policy of the *Register* to reveal authorship of any of the articles that appeared in the publication but he prepared to endure Hughes's assault "with as much composure as he could summon to his aid."[18] He had no fear of the young priest, but in Hughes he was to find an adversary worthy of respect. The discussion between Hughes and DeLancey lasted from the 14th of July through the 22nd of August, and attracted a great deal of attention among Catholics. One of the greatest results of the exchange was that for the first time, Hughes was introduced into the arena of theological conflict. By developing his writing and oratorical skills, Hughes was presenting himself to his coreligionists as the man to whom they could turn to in the defense and championing of their religion. Previously, his writings had been done on more of leisurely basis and were never signed. From the time of his encounter with DeLancey, Hughes made it his mission to answer and fight against every insult hurled at Catholicism. In October of 1829, Hughes attended the provincial council of Baltimore as an unofficial adviser, together with Father Hurley and the Philadelphia diocesan administrator, Father Matthews. In the course of the council, Bishop Conwell turned up at the proceedings, and while he did not actively participate, did consult on a regular basis with his episcopal brethren. He had informed the Holy See that Hughes was the fittest person in the diocese to succeed him as bishop; the powers to be favored the promotion of Patrick Kendrick, the president of a theological seminary in Bardstown, Kentucky. It was Kendrick that the council had advised should be named as coadjutor of the diocese with full powers of administration. It was not a slight to the ability of Hughes, rather, it was a stroke of good luck, as Hughes was already being considered for other Sees; Hughes's consecration, which was to come to fruition sooner rather than later, was a foregone conclusion. It is questionable as to whether or not Hughes was aware that Conwell had made the recommendation to have him promoted. In any event, Hughes continued the day to day parish work, visitations, sick calls, confessions, conversions, visitations, schools, asylums and other pastoral activities with an enthusiasm that prevented him from giving thought to a mitre or crozier.[19] Writing to his sister, Ellen, who had become Sister Angela of the Sisters of Charity of Emmitsburg, the busy Father Hughes writing on September 17th, 1829 addressed her growing perception of neglect.... "I am always distressed, my dear sister, when I perceive in your letters expressions accusing me of neglect toward you. It is true, if you were to judge my affection for you by the number of letters, you would have some reason for the suspicion; but I have explained it so often that, when you consider my situation and your own, you ought to make every allowance. I hope the time will come when I can write to you without risk of neglecting more important duties; but at present, and indeed at all times since I came to Philadelphia, I am like a servant who has a thousand masters at once."[20]

Francis Patrick Kendrick's appointment as the bishop of Philadelphia was officially announced on May 19th, 1830. He was consecrated at Bardstown by Bishop Flaget on the 6th of June. Kendrick was 32 years old at the time he became a bishop, six months younger than one of his soon to be priests, John Hughes. He, like Hughes, was Irish born. He was a native of Dublin and a graduate of the College of the Propaganda in Rome. Since the age of 24, he had held the position of superior of the theological seminary in Bardstown, Kentucky. He was a Vatican prodigy, a theologian by training and a cleric on the fast track. No study of the two men could have revealed greater contrast in substance and style. Kendrick was an academician, relieving the occasional confinement of the life of study with periodic missionary trips into the Kentucky hinterland. He was not a polemicist, and recoiled from the confrontational approach of dealing with religious questions in newspapers. Writing to Father Hughes just before his appointment, Kendrick confided that "I hope your occupations will leave you leisure to pen occasionally some similar productions, calculated to smooth the ruffled surface of the prejudiced mind."[21] Kendrick was referring to tract pieces Hughes had written in connection to the controversy with Dr. DeLancey. While Kendrick followed the traditional lead of the Catholic hierarchy of the time by not doing or saying anything that would exacerbate Protestant passions, he nonetheless was a solid and determined man under the deceptive veneer of an easygoing nature. He ultimately asserted his will over the trustees and congregants of St. Mary. While Hughes welcomed the coming of Kendrick, he was not about to acquiesce to the preferences of his new bishop with respect to ignoring the ever ready and abundant numbers of anti-Catholic antagonists. So much had Hughes now committed to the thrust and parry of engaging anti-Catholic enemies with the pen that it was to lead to an unfortunate incident, one not directly with the enemies of Catholicism, but with a fellow priest in the diocese of New York. In the maturation process of Hughes as priest and expositor and protector of the Catholic Faith, the "Cranmer" incident is not reflective in many ways of his better angels, for ultimately, as the events will reflect, his total emotional absorption in the heat of battle at times could result in a bitterness that was both destructive as well as truly alien to his makeup.

In November of 1829, a weekly publication by the name of *The Protestant* commenced publication in New York City. The establishment and launching of this enterprise had been given a solid endorsement by many ministers of the various Protestant denominations. Its purpose for existence was simple: to actively attack the Catholic Church at every conceivable point, and in doing so, condemn and denounce every manifestation of popery, its nuns, its priests, its ceremonies and its teachings. With no regard for either accuracy or decency, the material published proved so vile and scurrilous that some Protestant papers were forced to denounce it. Hughes decided to test the limits of *The Protestant*. Posing as a Protestant, Hughes set out to send in a series of exaggerated claims about the growing progress of Catholicism in various quarters under the name of "Cranmer." Hughes, no doubt thinking of the humorous aspects of his adventure plied *The Protestant* with overblown and false accounts of everything from the number of Masses being said to ceremonies which never took place, even a description of a supposed Jesuit academy in Cambria County, Pennsylvania, which was a figment of Hughes's imagination. *The Protestant* took the bait and frantically demanded more: "Our Philadelphia friend communicates his melancholy intelligence in a very Evangelical spirit of sensibility and fervor. We trust Cranmer will remember that his letters are sermons of momentous importance, and they are now read with intense and increasing interest by a rapidly augmenting host of Protestants of like spirit."[22] After Hughes had carried on this deception for some time, he finally threw off his mask and over the signature of "A Catholic," proceeded to excoriate the character of the Protestant paper: "I found that from the moment I spoke against Catholics, and adopted the signature of the coward, cruel but hypocritical Cranmer, I might write anything, however false (nay, the falser the better), and it was published under the sanction of your names. In a word, I could not find a line deep enough to fathom the editorial depravity of *The Protestant*."[23] The editors of *The Protestant* believed the letter sent by Hughes to be a forgery from a priest in the Diocese of New York. Hughes replied to the allegation by stating that he would offer a wager of $500.00 that there were at least four people in Philadelphia alone who had been regular contributors of the kind of trash that *The Protestant* had been in the habit of publishing. Hughes believed that his mission had been completed and while he felt a great sense of personal satisfaction over the affair, he was highly criticized by many Catholics who were angry at the level of duplicity Hughes had engaged in. One such person was a brother priest,

Father Thomas C. Levins of St. Patrick's Cathedral on Mott Street in New York City. Levins, a member of the Jesuit order, had immigrated from Ireland in 1822. Having served in the capacity of professor of Mathematics and Philosophy at Clongowes, the famous Jesuit School in Dublin, Levins had been part of the Jesuit community at Georgetown in Washington D.C. Coming to New York along with Father Joseph A. Schneller, both men acted as assistants to John Power, Vicar General of the New York Diocese and founder of the Catholic publication *The Truth Teller*.[24] Levins, an ill-tempered man, wrote a scathing reply to Hughes under the pen name of Fergus McAlpin. The both men exchanged acrimonious replies and counter replies for the better part of a year. In the end, it did not go a long way in winning and influencing friends for the young Hughes. At the close of the conflict, Hughes, in a reflective letter to his friend John Purcell, later to become Archbishop of Cincinnati, spoke of refusal, when in the right, of backing away from confrontation. This indeed was a quality of Hughes, but one possessed of the seeds of both dignified success as well as humiliating failure: "Experience has proved to *my* satisfaction that the dread of scandal, which usually restrains good men from defending themselves, is in its operation a kind of encouragement to that aggressive spirit which triumphs by its recklessness. If the birch had been applied to McAlpin's back ten years ago, it would not be necessary for me, as it is now to apply it. I have certainly been severe, and however the present affair may terminate, still I am confident that McAlpin will take care how he meddles with what does not immediately concern him hereafter."[25]

Bishop Kendrick was embarking on his first full visitation of the Diocese of Philadelphia. Accompanying him was Father Hughes, who was to have the privilege of preaching before his own parents in Chambersburg. The trip was exhaustive, bringing the two men to Bedford, Pittsburgh and Blairsville, as well as a stop in the Allegheny Mountains to spend time with the eminent Russian, Father Galitzin. A former nobleman and convert to Catholicism, Galitzin had founded a Catholic settlement in Loretto. In the aftermath of the visit, Hughes functioned as secretary to Bishop Kendrick.

The embers still burned at St. Mary's, and the trustees again attempted to subvert the peace. Kendrick, with Hughes unyieldingly by his side, placed the parish under interdict. The trustees relented and gave up their claim to the right of appointing pastors. This time Hughes scored a decisive victory against the trustees and against the trustee system. He set about building a new church, one whose title would be in the name of the bishop and whose organization would be without trustees or any of the other intrusive impediments that laymen had long imposed on the clergy. The design of the new building was to be done by the young architect, William Rodrigue, a man whose family and friendship was to bear abundant fruit for Hughes in the years to come. St. John's parish was dedicated in 1832. The opening of the new church with Hughes as pastor practically resulted in the abandonment of St. Mary's by parishioners. The new parish was heavily in debt, and coming to the rescue was one Mark Frenaye, a wealthy, middle-aged, West Indian born merchant, who was brought back to the "Faith" by Bishop DuBois, and as a result, saw a new role for himself in relation to his Catholic religion. Frenaye practically donated his entire fortune to pull the nascent parish out of the red. The pace of Hughes's priestly life and work increased with the new parish adding to the already numerous duties that had become an entrenched part of his day to day life. He accepted all in the spirit of good humor and dedication. He poured every ounce of his energy into the task of being a good and faithful pastor. In the midst of his work, he still found time for personal development and study, especially theology. He focused on the differences between Catholics and Protestants with laser like precision. He intuitively knew continued preparation for battle was a necessity, for the opportunity to engage was ever present. He was soon to be on the stage of conflict once again, but this time with a most formidable adversary. In his debates with the Presbyterian Reverend Dr. John Breckinridge, Hughes was not only going to stand toe to toe with the plumed knight of American Protestantism, he was also going to leave not a shred of doubt in the minds of anyone as to the right of Roman Catholicism to exist in the United States.

Chapter 4

Catholicism Comes Out of the Shadows

The circumstances around which John Hughes was to be catapulted onto the larger stage of theological controversy oddly enough was the result of an outbreak of disease. By the summer of 1832, the generally antagonistic relationship between Catholics and Protestants along the eastern seaboard of the United States was temporarily quieted due to of an outbreak of Asiatic cholera. While this virulent strain had never broken out anywhere in the Western Hemisphere, Americans watched with some trepidation as the disease spread into Europe, speculating that perhaps it would be brought to America's shore through the increase in numbers of arriving immigrants. When an outbreak occurred in Canada, it was logical to assume that it was the result of the large numbers of Irish immigrants making their way through Canadian ports of entry. Heightened fear stemmed from the belief that the United States was the ultimate destination for many of the Irish, so a series of quarantine laws were enacted to preempt immigrants from coming into New York. The laws neither prevented the immigrants nor the cholera from making its way south. By the early summer, New York City had become infested. By midsummer, the contagion had travelled as far as Philadelphia, and the cholera struck quickly and fatally. Unlike previous plagues of yellow fever, which was better understood medically, the violent cramps, diarrhea and vomiting of cholera often brought its victims to the door of death within a matter of hours. The people who had the means to do so moved from the city into the more remote country regions, where the scattered human population minimized the chances for exposure. Observers of the situation concluded that only because of the influx of immigrants, generally forced into living conditions that were crowded together and lacking in the proper hygienic amenities such as clean water and sewerage, was the disease able to speedily and fatally take hold. Protestant preachers, pointing to the moral degeneracy to be found among the outsiders, were quick to point out that it was an avenging God enacting retribution against such people for their falling from grace and their manner of living. As conditions in Philadelphia worsened, many Protestant congregations locked their doors and vacated their churches. Catholic clergy on the other hand remained in their churches, continuing with the saying of Mass and the normal daily activities of parish life, and more than ever, increased sick calls to the dying and burying the mounting numbers of the dead. In one instance, Bishop Kendrick gave permission to turn St. Augustine's Church into an infirmary and the Sisters of Charity from Emmitsburg ventured into the sick zones to tend to the sick and dying. The priests of the diocese in many instances acted with the nuns, administering medicines needed for those who had been stricken. The valor of the Catholic Church did not go unnoticed in the press. Rather than fleeing, the nuns and priests stayed behind to do their jobs, and their selfless effort became a source of embarrassment for members of the Protestant community. John Hughes made sure that the sacramental life of St. Joseph's continued in an uninterrupted fashion. He shared the work of assisting those in hospital as well as maintenance of a vehicle to be at the ready each and every day for transport to sick calls, many of which came during the night.[1] Ezra Styles Ely, editor of the sectarian newspaper *Philadelphian,* commented how the steadfastness of the Catholic religious communities during the crisis was only possible because Catholic priests and nuns had no wives or husbands by law, and no children to be concerned about. They were, in effect, not bringing home the potential to spread disease. Ely went on to say that while the actions of the Catholic clergy and nuns were commendable, there was no evidence showing that their fidelity was better or any different than anyone else. No doubt born of the striking inactivity with respect to his own faith community, Ely was attempting to salve the bruised conscience of Protestants. His veiled slur against the nuns and priests who did not marry "by law" roused in Hughes the impulse to attack. Hughes started by pointing out that Ely himself had been absent from the city, and that while the Catholic clergy "had no right to take to themselves credit of doing more than they were bound to do,"[2] Hughes stated if Protestants were consistent about what they were actually preaching, they should have been among their people guarding them "against the delusions of that ministry which they are accustomed to denounce as the ministry of the Antichrist."[3] The skirmishing between Hughes and Ely continued into the fall, with Hughes forwarding blistering counters to the *United States Gazette*, criticizing Ely for use of words like "Romish" to describe the Catholic religion. In another sharp rebuke to Protestant inaction during the height of the cholera epidemic, Hughes fired back that Protestant ministers were "remarkable for their pastoral solicitude so long as the flock is healthy."[4] For the Presbyterian minister, John Breckinridge, Hughes proved too much to pass by. Breckinridge had been a close and watchful observer of this brash and bold upstart priest, and he chose now to challenge him in a series of theological debates, no doubt desirous of trimming the sails of the Catholic clergy in the process, a group whose collective intelligence he questioned. Breckinridge, as Hughes was to soon discover, was no pulpit pounding sensationalist, no country carnival barker. He was born on Independence Day, 1797, the same year in which his soon to be opponent had been born across the water. His father had served as Attorney General of the United States under President Thomas Jefferson, and young Breckinridge attended and graduated from Princeton in 1818. It was during his student years that be commenced the association with Presbyterianism. Initially intended for the legal profession, he chose the ministry instead. After becoming licensed to preach in 1822, became chaplain of the House of Representatives. Later pastoral assignments brought him to Kentucky and Baltimore, before being reassigned as secretary to the Presbyterian Board of Education. In 1836, he was appointed to a professorship at the Princeton Theological Seminary. A strict proponent of Calvinistic Presbyterianism, Breckinridge was an able preacher and even abler debater.[5] In the wake of the harsh rebukes that Hughes had been hurling at the Protestant ministry, Breckinridge advised that he would meet any priest or bishop in the arena of discussion concerning the two traditions. Hughes rose to the challenge and as word of a Protestant-Catholic debate spread, tremendous interest was generated on the part of ordinary people. Breckenridge, no doubt fully confident of his prowess as a debater, attempted to have the first encounter be in the form of an oral exchange. Hughes, while appreciably more confident in his abilities with respect to oral argumentation, was still aware of the great deficiencies of his own education and would not risk this type of exchange against one who had been grounded as Breckinridge had been in the Classics. It was decided that the contest was to start as an exchange in newspapers, with each of the opponents responding to the essays of the other. As there was no such Catholic outlet in Philadelphia, Hughes, with the help of the Augustinian Father Nicholas O'Donnell, founded the *Catholic Herald*. Writing to Breckinridge on October 3rd, 1832, Hughes, having accepted the challenge, expressed surprise in "that you seem to regret that your antagonist is not an accredited or responsible authority on the subject, and hence you say there are priests and bishops, etc. We are prepared to meet any of them on the broad field of this vital and important discussion and *hereby* make this disposition known. I am equally ready to accept this challenge – let it be only conducted in a spirit of Christian Charity, and sincere inquiry after truth. Of course it will be necessary to define certain rules and conditions by which we may understand ourselves and each other in the discussion of the question."[6] On October 13th, Breckinridge replied "Sir, allow me to say, that it gives me hearty pleasure to find you disposed, in a manly form, to meet the question at issue between Protestants and Romanists, while at the same time I fully respond to the wish expressed in your letter that any controversy which may hereafter be undertaken, may be conducted in a sincere inquiry after the truth."[7] Hughes, no doubt wincing at the use of the appellation of "Romanist," nonetheless determined to stick with the promise he had made with respect to decorum. The two men agreed that the discussion was to proceed as follows:

> "The parties shall write and publish alternately, in the weekly paper called the *Presbyterian*, and a Roman Catholic paper to be furnished by the First of January, it being understood that the communications shall be published after the following plan: one party opening in the first week, the other party replying in the next week, and every piece to be republished in the immediate succeeding number of the Roman Catholic paper. The communications not to exceed four columns in the *Presbyterian*, nor to continue beyond six months, without consent of the parties."[8]

Hughes was designated to lead off and on January 21st, 1833, his first essay on the "Rule of Faith" was in print, and the battle was joined between the two protagonists. Hughes started out in a conciliatory tone, and opened the discussion with observations tinged with a touch of sorrow as to how and why the great divisions among Christians had grown so wide and so pronounced. "I judge no man – be the sect or denomination to which he belongs what it may. When we reflect that there was a time when the multitude of believers had but one heart and one soul, and contrast that period with the conflict of opinions, and the rivalship of creeds which has produced the present distracted condition of the Christian family, the lover of truth may find enough to make him weep for charity."[9] Conciliation however soon reverted to directing the attack against what Hughes believed to be the heart of Protestant error, namely, the Bible alone as the practical rule of faith. "The question then is this: Is the *Bible alone* the practical rule of faith, established by Christ, to guide us in matters of religion and to determine disputes in his Church? If it is not, then it will follow, that the whole Protestant system, that is, the system of all who adopt the Bible alone to "guide them in the matters of religion" hinges on a principle which is vicious and defective."[10] Hughes then laid out ten articles with respect to his arguments against the authority of the Bible, challenging Breckinridge to refute each article. Hughes, always the ready combatant in the face of the common anti-Catholic bigotry of the age, peppered his challenge with the admonition that "the cause of truth required that you should meet my arguments and refute them, article for article. What course you will adopt to accomplish this, it is difficult for me to conceive. But I am satisfied that our readers will not be contented with the sliding system of controversial tactics by which the opponents of the true religion, are accustomed to "slur the notes" of an argument, which they *cannot answer.*"[11] No less aggressive in his reply on February 2nd, nor disposed to extended niceties, Breckinridge proceeded to focus his main attacks against the validity of Catholic tradition and the centrality of the Pope with respect to the practical rule of faith. Referring to the Pope as the "judge of controversies," Breckinridge retorted that "If you have an infallible, visible judge of controversy, how do you get at the proof of his infallibility? Is he not appointed by Christ? You say he is. Then you find the proof of it in sacred Scriptures of course. How then do you interpret those Scriptures in discovering that there is such a judge? Not infallibility, for the existence of any infallible judge is yet to be proved. And as regards his existence you are left, as you must admit, to decide from Scripture by your own unaided reason. Can you then claim any more certainty of your opinion than we for ours?"[12] Citing the many conflicting interpretations of Catholic doctrine as viewed through different Church fathers, Councils, Papal Bulls, Decrees, etc., Breckinridge excoriated the notion of non-Biblical sources with respect to the rule of faith: "Your rule of faith requires you, as your oath of office binds you, to interpret "un-written traditions" and the Bible according to the "unanimous consent of the fathers." Now, I ask, is there any such unanimous consent? If not, how can your rule be applied? If there be, will you make it appear?"[13]

In all of the American Republic's relatively brief history, no discussion between two such persons, a Roman Catholic priest and a Presbyterian representative of mainline American Protestant thought, had ever taken place. The interest generated in this initial exchange was unprecedented with respect to the Catholic community, for here, for the first time, a member of the Catholic clergy was assuming the pointed role of defending in public the Catholic religion against the overwhelming prejudice that existed against it in America since the earliest days of the English colonial enterprise. Prior to the opening of this momentous debate, the closest friends of Hughes had begged him to forgo taking on Breckinridge and, in effect, the American Protestant establishment. Hughes however could not allow the aggregate "insults" against his Faith to pass without a challenge, and while there were Catholics as well as Protestants who were no doubt unable to fully grasp the fine points of theology, something transformational was taking place as the result of this exchange. Catholics were coming to realize that their belief system had an undeniable right to profess itself as any other, and Protestants were coming to understand that there existed in America a living Catholic Church, a Church asserting itself both intellectually as well as socially. Hughes was not going to waste the opportunity to attack Protestantism root and branch, and in his reply to Breckinridge on the 13th of February, 1833 remonstrated that "My first argument against the Protestant Rule of Faith was, *that Christ never appointed it.* The reasons by which I supported this argument were simple *facts.* It is a fact, that the Bible alone, interpreted by each individual for himself, is the (nominal) rule of faith adopted by Protestants. It is a fact that Christ never appointed this rule; – because he never wrote any part of the Old or New Testament himself; – he never commanded any part to be written by his apostles. It is a *fact,* that what constitutes the Bible (according to the Protestant canon of Scripture) was not complete until the close of the *first century;* and consequently, it is a fact, that the Protestant rule of faith did not exist in the *first century,* and is therefore not the rule that which *Christ* established. I call upon you to deny one single proposition here stated as a fact."[14] To be sure that the piling had been driven deep into the ground, Hughes, with barely hidden sarcasm, redefined what the actual question of the exchange should be: "The Protestant Rule of Faith. It cries out for a defender – for one who will prove it to be *"Infallible; established by Christ; competent to guide us in matters of religion; and to determine disputes in his Church.*"[15] Breckinridge, proving himself as much a brawler in the ring as anybody, castigated Catholicism as a compendium of corrupt practices: "once more, *the effect of your rule of faith is to corrupt the worship of God, and to engender abundant superstitions.* Idolatry (excuse the word), is enthroned in the temple of God, by the bulls of popes and the decrees of Councils; and is practically illustrated every day in the worship of the church. The spirituality of religion is lost amidst a crowd of images and relics; of intervening saints and human inventions: and ignorance perpetuates what your erring rule has legalized. Need I point you to exorcisms and incantations, to prayers to the saints, and worship of the Virgin Mary, to holy water, the baptism of bells, to pilgrimages and penances, and the crowd of superstitions which are encouraged in your church in confirmation of my statements?"[16] Driving the sword deeper into the flesh, Breckinridge mockingly asked the question: "Who would believe it, if it had not been seen, that in the nineteenth century of the Christian era, there is a great anniversary day, set apart in "Rome, the mother and mistress of churches," for blessing all the horses and asses and other beasts of the great city, whilst the same pontiff who sanctions such a system, publicly denounces Bible Societies, as the organizations and servants of the devil."[17]

The combat between Hughes and Breckinridge stretched on, taking on nastier and more antagonistic turns as discussion progressed. Breckinridge's undeviating tactic was to shred the superstitions, immorality and cruelties of the Roman Catholic Church. Hughes steadily countered by acknowledging the past sins of the "true" Church, and then acting as if Protestantism was a non-entity.[18] As the battering continued through the spring and early summer, Hughes, while unquestionably emerging as a true defender of the Catholic Faith, was simultaneously incurring the mounting disapproval not only of Bruté, who was virtually acting as his source of material to counter the Breckinridge onslaught, but an equally disapproving Bishop Kendrick. This became increasingly evident as the exchange grew more strident. Writing toward the end of March, 1833, Breckinridge expressed to Hughes "That it is hard work, you find, to meet and parry stubborn facts, especially when your own authors and formularies are turned against you. No wonder your defense struggles in the greatness of the way, and like a wounded snake, drags its slow length along. I regret to see that you grow *less courteous,* as well as more feeble and prolix; and it would seem that these qualities keep pace with each other, in the progress of the discussion."[19] Both unrelenting and unrepentant, Hughes replied: "The Protestant rule of faith supposes that the Scriptures are *plain and obvious* in their meaning. And yet, – the *plea* for the Reformation and the cry of the Reformers, was that the *whole Catholic Church has been mistaken* as the true meaning of this same book; – which was so plain withal, that *every* Protestant with ten months education, may take it up and "read as he runs!" – and that every such Protestant is bound to believe, that his crude conceptions of its meaning, make him wiser and more infallible, then all of the Councils, Fathers, teachers, pastors and people of all the ages of the Christian Church!!!"[20]

In a letter to Father Bruté, dated April 5th, 1833, Hughes wrote of the positive aspects of this controversy with respect to Protestant conversions to Catholicism: "There are some encouraging circumstances connected with this controversy. There are no less than three converts under instruction in this church now, in consequence, *as they say,* of its perusal – one a Baptist, one an Episcopalian and one a Duncanite Presbyterian, who was moved to pity the Church by the language in which her minister warned the "flock" not to venture inside of St. John's, nor listen to the sophistical lectures. The famous Parson McCalla has paid me two or three visits, without disclosing any other intention than a professed desire to know the real doctrine of the Church, and the book from which he might learn it. I have no anticipations in reference to him: but God may improve his heart and head, which have been those of a fanatic, to a better knowledge of the truth."[21] The discussions heightened in acrimony as spring turned into summer. As the days waxed warmer, the two men continued hurling words at each other, quoting Church Fathers, theologians, Scripture, Confessions and Decrees. One would reply to the other that the arguments put forward were inaccurate and distorted. One significant consequence of this behavior was a decrease in interest on the part of the general public. In the absence of a face to face confrontation, even the most enthusiastic followers were growing weary of the heavy duty theological lines of argument. Hughes however kept the sledge hammer in full swing, writing on May 22nd in response to an inaccurate statement made regarding an excerpt from a Papal bull that had been issued by Pope Innocent VIII concerning the extirpation of the heretical Vaudois, Hughes frustratingly told Breckinridge "I cannot pass from one quotation to another of your letters, without being *pained* at the necessity you impose on me, of exposing the ignorance of the authors you cite, or your dishonesty in quoting them. Even in your last letter whilst you effect to be greatly incensed at my charge on this head, and require me to apologize for my "insolence," you are detected in new falsifications."[22] At the start of this whole enterprise, it was Hughes who had accepted the challenge from Breckinridge to engage in a discussion of the differences between Catholicism and Protestantism. Hughes, now flushed with anger after months of the repeated attempts of his opponent to twist, distort, vilify and blacken the name of his Catholic Faith, threw down another gauntlet. In the same reply of May 22nd, Hughes told Breckinridge that should he want an apology for any past insolence, this is what the apology would be: "I will meet you before the General Assembly, or in any public hall in the city, on any day you feel proper to name, and convict your letters of having added or "omitted" words, "changed" the punctuation," and so falsified the authorities – in presence of any number of gentlemen and ladies who may think proper to attend. I hope this alternative will be sufficient atonement, for what you are pleased to call my insolence."[23] In his response, Breckinridge likened

Hughes to "renowned Ecclesiastic bullies of New York," who are now expanding their course and vulgar railleries against the Bible and the bible and the friends of Christ; who are edifying us much without intending it; and have the effect which the great critic of antiquity assigns to the stage, that of *purifying the heart by pity and terror.*"[24] Knowing full well that the General Assembly to which Hughes referred to as a venue for a public discussion had already adjourned, Breckinridge reminded Hughes that his "courage was not equal to a public meeting six months ago, or the whole ground of controversy might long since have been traversed."[24] With stinging sarcasm, Breckenridge concluded his correspondence with an extract from a letter to Pope Paul III expressing the hope that "you are chosen to *restore the name of Christ forgotten by the nations* and even by *us the clergy,* that hereafter it may live in our hearts, and appear in our actions; to heal our diseases, to reduce the flock of Christ into one sheepfold, to remove from us the vengeance of God, *which we deserve,* which is now ready to fall upon us, which now hangs over our heads!"[25] The picture it gave of the state of the church, left no room for comment. As if foretelling the future with respect to the Catholic religion, Hughes, on June 21st, confidently predicted to Breckinridge that "a new era has come in our country. The American people will promptly see 'who the serpent is' (to use your own illustration,) that stings the bosom which warms it. They will henceforth know where to send their children for education, and when to contribute in generous, and abused confidence, to build the Schools, Convents, and Chapels, that are to train the children to call their parents *heretics*; and are arising to re-establish a religion which never did, never will and never can permit a free government or religious toleration. The people are awake or awaking; and you must change your system or lose your prize."[26]

By September, the correspondence between Hughes and Breckinridge had stretched out over eight long months, and Breckinridge informed his adversary that he was required to leave the city for a period of time for the purpose travelling through the country. He did however renew the challenge to Hughes to engage in an oral debate upon his return. Hughes would not accept the challenge. Responding to Breckinridge, he advised that "if your business carries you abroad, you are free to discontinue when you please, and to resume when you find it convenient to do so. But you must not deprive me of my right to return the arrow which you shoot – in retreating. When you return you may resume the contest, and I shall be prepared to receive you."[27]

There is little question that Bishop Kendrick was not at all happy with any of these proceedings. During one of the intervals involving the back and forth exchange between Hughes and Breckinridge, the question was debated as to whether or not Kendrick had actually told the Catholic Faithful not to read any of the correspondence; Kendrick denied ever having any statement in support of that charge. For Hughes, it was a clear cut case of standing up for the beliefs of the Church. Catholicism was still very much a religion under attack in the United States, and the level of anti-Catholicism in the normal course of events was intense. Writing to Bruté in early March, 1833, Hughes making reference to the controversy with Breckinridge stated that "I was bound to engage."[28]

In his own assessment of the manner in which the discussions progressed, Hughes reflected that "it is not for me to say one word in the way of opinion as to the manner in which my opponent sustained the Protestant Rule of Faith, or acquitted himself in the arguments and authorities adduced to disprove the Catholic principle of religious guidance. But for some months back there has been a considerable undertone of dissatisfaction among the better informed Protestants generally, not excepting Presbyterians themselves. They had never suspected the strength of the Catholic position on the Rule of Faith nor the weakness of their own. And in the mood of feeling, they ascribed the sufferings of the cause to the incompetence of the advocate. Even some of the Protestant clergy did not hesitate to say that Mr. Breckinridge was not "the man" that should have been selected; that he had no business to engage in such a discussion without being authorized by those whom he undertook to represent."[29] With the battle temporarily over, it was now left for those who had followed the discussions to assess the results. For Catholics generally, and Hughes particularly, the encounter proved a great success. In Pennsylvania at least, there had been no Catholic who had yet come along who was able to defend the Faith against her adversaries on fair ground; this part of the equation had been irrevocably changed by Hughes. From the moment Hughes accepted the challenge to stand up for Catholics, he was perceived as their defender and ever after would be viewed as their protector in times of crisis. With his writing ability, Hughes had literally turned on its head the notion advanced by Breckinridge that the Roman Catholic clergy was a collection of unintelligent agents of the Pope, bent on preserving their divine power through fear and superstition. More importantly, Hughes demonstrated a courage and skill throughout, which was held in high esteem not only by his own coreligionists, but by members of the Protestant community as well. Amazingly, Hughes came to be shown a respect by the Protestants of Philadelphia in a way no Catholic priest had known for years. Hughes, from his earliest days as a priest, was no stranger to religious controversy. In the past, his participation had always been the focused defense of his own creed, not too attack others. In summarizing his role, Hughes affirmed how "I have had intercourse with society of all denominations; I have preached nearly every Sunday, oftentimes in controversy, when hundreds of Protestants were present; and I venture to assert that I have not done one action or used one expression, in the pulpit or out of it, to warrant the charge of malignity. I have wounded no man's feelings; I have injured no man's character... I am proud to believe, and have reason to believe, that, though a Catholic and a priest, I stand as high in public, even Protestant estimations as Mr. Breckinridge himself."[30] it was an unusual statement to make given the American religious climate of 1833, but nonetheless, Hughes had undeniably earned the right to make it. It was during the first engagement with Breckinridge that Hughes was under consideration for the bishopric of the See of Cincinnati. The other candidate being looked at by Rome was John Purcell. Charleston's Bishop England was in Rome at the time and was being pressured by his brother bishops to use whatever influence he could to expedite the filling of this episcopal vacancy. In England's interviews with the Cardinal Prefect of the Propaganda, England was asked if there was any light he could shed with respect to a quality or attribute that might make one candidate better for the appointment than the other. England, neither willing nor prepared to tip the balance in favor of either Hughes or Purcell hesitatingly responded that because Hughes was more of a self-made man, the people of a Western diocese like Cincinnati might find him a more acceptable replacement than Purcell. By a misunderstanding in the translation, the Cardinal Prefect advised England the next day about the matter of Cincinnati being settled. "As soon as I told the Cardinals what you said about *Fr. Purcell's* being a self-made man, they agreed upon him unanimously."[31]

England was loath to comment further upon the obvious error, and the Cardinal was never made aware of the blunder he had made. In any event, believing that silence was the best policy and that the Holy Spirit had ultimately intervened in deciding the question as to who would take over Cincinnati was concerned, John Purcell became bishop, but John Hughes was not to be far behind in the receipt of miter and crozier. In the meanwhile, Hughes was again to cross swords with Breckinridge, this time in the format originally desired by the latter... an oral debate. For many observers, the sometimes unpleasant experienced between Hughes and Breckinridge during their first encounter would have been a deterrent against a return engagement. Additionally, support in Catholic ecclesiastic circles did not at all seem well disposed to engaging Breckinridge again. Hughes however had different ideas. He could not find it within himself to retreat from the prospect of answering the charges leveled against his Church by a man, who made no bones in public about disparaging in a most distasteful way the Pope, Catholics and Catholic religious practice. The origin of the second discussion was the result of the formation in Philadelphia of the Union Literary and Debating Institute. The organization was composed of members of both the Catholic and Protestant religions, and Hughes was made both an honorary member and invited to attend meetings. In January of 1835, the group decided to adopt as a proposition for discussion *"Is the Roman Catholic Religion In any or all of its principles and Doctrines, inimical to Civil or Religious Liberty?"* Hughes was asked if he would prepare a talk to address the group on the question for the evening of January 22nd. When Hughes arrived in the hall on the appointed evening, he was met by the Reverend McCalla, a cohort of Breckinridge.[32] At this juncture, the society adopted a resolution to the effect that Hughes was not to present the lecture as originally planned, but could debate Reverend McCalla, if he chose to do so. The whole ploy had been orchestrated with the idea of dragging Hughes into a public debate. On January 21st, Breckinridge had composed and forwarded to Hughes from New York the following letter:

Sir:

I have shortly been informed that you are expected to address a society to-morrow evening on a question of which the following is the substance, viz: "Whether the Roman Catholic Religion is favorable to Civil and Religious Liberty?"

I write a few lines in order to say that I will meet you, on the evening of the 29th instant, before the same society, Providence permitting, on that question; – or if that be not agreeable to you, in any other place where this vital question may be fully discussed before our fellow-citizens.

As I shall not be present, I suggest that you will yourself make the necessary suggestions to the society to-morrow evening, and give me as early a reply as convenient. I can conceive of only one reason for your refusing, and I hope time has overcome that.

> I remain your obedient servant,
> John Breckinridge[33]

Hughes, enraged at both the presence of McCalla and the impertinence of Breckinridge resolved to answer the challenge because, if he failed to do so, "the trump of triumphant falsehood would proclaim my defeat, and ascribe it to a wrong motive."[34]

Opposed to the last engagement between Hughes and Breckinridge, the venue for the oral debate had taken a drastically different turn. In this round, the Protestant clergy was out for blood, and Protestant papers such as the *Presbyterian* and *The Protestant Vindicator* were already proclaiming prior to the debate that Hughes had not only been annihilated and pulverized, but that he had also fled the scene. This of course was far from the truth. The meeting with McCalla on January the 22nd was to establish the meaning of certain terms and conditions with respect to the debate:

Definitions

I. Religious Doctrines

Those tenets of the faith and morals, which a denomination teaches as having been revealed by the Almighty God.

II. Religious Liberty

The right of each individual to worship God according to the dictates of his conscience, without injuring or invading the rights of others.

III. Civil Liberty

The absolute rights of an individual restrained only for the preservation of order in society.[35]

On the 29th of January, Breckinridge, the editor of The *Protestant Vindicator*, the Reverend Dr. W.C. Brownlee and other members of the Protestant clergy were present at the Union Literary Hall. The conditions as previously set forth were accepted by all parties, and shortly thereafter, Hughes made his entrance. The debate was opened and the balance of the evening witnessed a polite and courteous discussion between Father Hughes and Reverend Breckinridge. Again, the two men affirmed the debate topics, starting off with "*Is the Catholic Religion, in any or all of its Principles and Doctrines, opposed* to *Civil or Religious liberty.*" A total of six evenings were to be devoted to this topic, to be followed by another six evenings of discussion on "*Is the Presbyterian Religion, in any or all of its Principles and Doctrines opposed to Civil or Religious Liberty?*" Each of the two men were entitled to bring a total of one hundred people as listeners. A short-hand writer was to be present to impartially record the debate between the two men. The final major point was that the only two participants could be Hughes and Breckinridge. If anyone believed that amity between the participants was to be long lived, that notion was completely shattered from the opening of Breckinridge's first speech: "I enter on the discussion of this important question, I wish to say to this society, that I hold in my hand a Roman Catholic paper, published in New York called "*The New York Weekly Register* and *Catholic Diary*, No.21, Vol. III, Feb. 21st, 1835" – which purports, in a letter signed R.C.W., to give as true report of our preliminary discussion held in this hall some evenings since – This letter is a tissue of uncandid statements, and is most scandalously and injuriously *false*.[36] In reply, Hughes set the record straight by maintaining that "the Society were witnesses to what occurred, and competent to *specify* the pretended misstatements. If they cannot do this, it is unreasonable to require the reparation demanded. For this, neither is it necessary that the gentlemen be made acquainted with the name of the writer; and the gentleman's *demand* to have that name given up to him, is a pretty fair example of what Presbyterians understand by civil and religious liberty."[37] That Breckinridge was looking for the moment to engage his opponent face to face was well known from the very start of the exchange between the two men back in 1833. Hughes, at first reluctant, decided it was neither in his nor his Church's best interest to demonstrate any timidity in the face of what would surely be a more intensive and caustic engagement, when both men could stare each other in the eyes before their respective supporters. On the evening of Breckinridge's second affirmative address, he wasted no time in boring down hard on the chance to display the kind of accepted prejudice and hostility common to mainstream American Protestantism: "And here allow me thus early in the debate, to say, that nothing but the love of liberty as an American, and of truth as a protestant Christian, could induce me to subject my feelings to the course and ill-bred impertinence of a priesthood, whose temper and treatment towards other men, alternate between servility to their spiritual sovereigns and oppression of their unhappy subjects. I can and will bear for the sake of the *great cause* – whatever may be necessary, though, thank God, I am not forced to do it either as a minion of the Pope or the subject of arrogant and vulgar *Jesuitism*.[38] Hughes, dropping the anvil from the highest point of contempt and sarcasm down onto Breckinridge's head retorted: "Do you not, sir, pity the gentleman? The Chesterfield of the Presbyterian Church, – the magister elegantarium – to be exposed to the retorts of a Catholic priest! But, "for sake of the great cause" he is willing to be a martyr. – Still it is hard to have his fine, delicate feelings exposed to such rude treatment! He ought, however, to remember, that aiming at the immortality of an author, he must be prepared to encounter the trials in which his ambition has exposed him. When he uses language in reference to his present position, which is a violation of the most common politeness, he cannot expect that it will be allowed to pass unnoticed."[39] Further, Hughes laid down a fundamental belief of his concerning the obligations of citizens, religious and civil with respect to the nation, countering an often cited charge of Breckinridge, and Protestants in general, that the Pope is the one to whom Catholics must give their primary obedience: "I had laid down as a principle, that the man, who, as a citizen, refuses to discharge the duties lawfully imposed on him, by that relation: or, as a member of a Church, refuses to comply with the regulations *of the religious society to which he belongs* "by appeal to his pretended natural right, would be justly regarded as unworthy to participate in the privilege of either: viz. of the government or of the church, to which he belonged."[40] Hughes even, with characteristic logic and the methodically precise ability to dissect and then refute many of his opponent's arguments, did not fare as well in this format with Breckinridge as with writing. The reality of the debates is that many of the city's most intelligent and better informed citizens did not patronize them, henceforth, the meetings were populated largely by the lower classes of both religions. While this group may not have followed the fine points of the complex theological arguments, they were certainly able to detect a slanderous accusation or falsehood against a person. Hughes was loath to have to appear before such a group, and while he hated having to carry on with the kind of audience in attendance, it did not deter him from pulling into minute particles and destroying every wrong-headed argument advanced by Breckinridge. There was another advantage that Breckinridge utilized to great advantage, that is, Protestant clergy utilized in their homiletics the powerful repetitiveness of the spoken word to create vivid impressions and images in the minds of their congregants. When, for example, Breckinridge repeated arguments that had already been disposed of by Hughes or brought up irrelevant questions, Hughes would not dignify this kind of rhetoric with a response. To the uneducated listener, Hughes's silence was interpreted as having been vanquished, whereas Hughes was merely refusing to entertain points, which to him would have appeared redundant, trite or merely stupid. The use of a stenographer was to have the benefit of the complete and accurate exchange between the two men, but it was revealed that upon examination of the stenographer's report of the debate, it was both incomplete as well as full of errors. A proposal was introduced to allow each of the participants to review their speeches and submit them for publication as well as to their adversary. Each was allowed, after review, to amplify on topics covered as well as initiate new ones for discussion. The result of this allowance was a proliferation of writing on the part of both men, which rendered the cost of printing prohibitive. The Union Literary Society urged both economy as well as expedience govern the reproduction of the body of the discussions between the two men. Hughes was the first to concede, and offered to cut the additional work short with publication of only twenty-four original speeches, twelve on each of the two questions. This format was finally agreed upon, and the work was sold by the Institute to Carey, Lea and Blanchard of Philadelphia, who in 1836 published the following title: *"A Discussion of the Question, Is the Roman Catholic Religion, in any or in all its Principles or Doctrines, inimical to Civil or Religious Liberty and of the question, is the Presbyterian Religion in any or in all its Principles and Doctrines inimical to Civil or Religious Liberty? By the Reverend John Hughes of the Roman Catholic Church and the Reverend John Breckinridge of the Presbyterian Church.*"[41] In spite of the pointed attacks Hughes made against Breckinridge, his Presbyterian beliefs and American Protestantism in general, Hughes had achieved an unprecedented respect and popularity with the Philadelphia Protestant establishment. He was accorded a respect and deference, prompted greatly by the fact that he had conducted himself with civility and great decorum in his recent encounter. He was recognized as a man of great intelligence and ability to communicate. More importantly, his personality appealed to the "American" dimension of the average Protestant of the era, who believed Hughes, more than anything else, had displayed great courage and fearlessness in defense of his Church and his religious beliefs. He was the recipient of dinner invitations from prominent members of the community, and in this setting proved witty, affable and ever solid in representing Roman Catholicism to the broader populous. In the right company, he was well able to sing a song, and his own parishioners grew in increased devotion to their pastor and champion. There was a downside however to the acclaim of having crossed swords with the plumed knight of Protestantism. While seeing Hughes in admiring eyes, there was no getting around the fact that his admirers were poor. St. Joseph's parish was heavily in debt, and Hughes was not able to see his way past the insurmountable financial mountain that he found himself having to climb. Hughes had heard that the Catholics of Mexico were rich, and so he determined to learn Spanish and strike out to that country to find financial aid for his strapped parish at home. When word of this effort became known, the parishioners, for fear of losing their pastor, launched a series of intensive campaigns to do whatever was in their power mitigate the crushing debt of the parish.[42] There were other problems besides the financial ones, problems of a more serious nature in that they involved Hughes's ecclesiastic superior, Bishop Kendrick, who never masked his negative view with respect to such distasteful public displays involving the Catholic clergy. Just as the correspondence war between his priest and Breckinridge, Kendrick tried to do everything in his power, short of actually ordering Hughes to refrain from participating in the debates. He forbade the *Catholic Herald* from providing coverage of the debates, and allegedly, at least according to people like Breckinridge, had issued directives for Catholics to not attend any of the debates, though Kendrick privately stated that he had never issued such a directive. In appreciation for what John Hughes had done during the course of the debates, the Catholic members of the Union Literary Society presented him with a beautifully bound edition of the debates as well as a piece of plate. In the gracious letter of acceptance that Hughes wrote back to the society, he made reference to the importance, in his mind, of accepting the challenge of debating by writing that: "The people require only the correct information, and, so far as I was able, I deemed it a public duty to impart that information on the exciting question of civil and religious liberty."[43] Hughes further reflected on the lack of support of the publication on the part of those who held the anti-Catholic position, in that they were ultimately not interested in truth: "I believe that good has resulted from the effort, and as a proof I mention the fact that the book which has grown out of this discussion finds no patronage among the anti-Catholic crusaders who provoked its publication. It contains both sides of the question of civil and religious liberty; – their doctrines and our doctrines – their history and our history; and if they are sincere in their pretended zeal for the enlightenment of the public mind, let them aid to circulate the work among their adherents. Their refusal to do so shows that they feel their position, and are afraid of the light."[44]

The effects of the Hughes-Breckinridge encounters in the years between 1833 and 1836 were many and widespread. The Reverend W.C. Brownlee was so enamored of the Philadelphia experience that he raced back to New York to try out the same topics on a New York audience. Bishop Kendrick, ever conscious of the need to maintain peace and decorum at all cost, issued directives with respect to how the crowds of Irish Catholics who showed up to hear the debates were to act, but to no avail. On the night of the actual debate, a fight broke out and the hall was severely damaged. Bishop England commented favorably on the debates in the *Catholic Miscellany*, saying Breckinridge's attempt to slander Hughes could be likened to "some men who, while in a state of inebriety, imagine everyone about them to be under the influence of liquor but themselves."[45] While some may have viewed the conflict between Hughes and Breckinridge as long and pedantic, the reality of the Protestant "gentleman," come to put the ignorant foreign priest in his place and winding up battered in the exchange, was lost on nobody. John Hughes was not a theologian, though he defended the doctrines and history of the Catholic tradition with zeal and intelligence. While it is true he had immeasurable help from Simon Bruté with respect to formulation of many of his arguments, it was Hughes who ultimately stood in the ring to take the hard and at times vicious blows of not just one anti-Catholic, but of an entire anti-Catholic establishment. In the history of the American Republic up to that point in time, if Catholicism was not under interdiction, it had been repressed for fear of inciting Protestant sensibilities. If toleration and religious freedom was to mean more than just words, it was Hughes who pulled the carpet out from under the elephant sitting on the full exercise of both. Some would make the claim that it wasn't that Hughes was the better of the two men, rather, that Breckinridge was merely not the right man to take on the task at hand. One could argue for the correctness of this viewpoint; however, it would falsely obscure the reality of two resounding points no longer at issue in the fabric work of American religious life: 1.) The Catholic Church had emerged from the cover of darkness in American society, shedding its second class position not only in the minds of its own people, but in the minds of Protestants as well and 2.) John Hughes was the American Catholic Churchman who was in the forefront of this movement. Another development of greater consequence to Hughes was gaining ground, that is, his being considered for promotion to bishop. He had been previously considered for the Sees of Cincinnati as well as Pittsburg and Philadelphia, but fate was to bring Hughes to a very different kind of episcopal stage. In April of 1837, the Council of Baltimore forwarded to Rome the names of John Hughes, the Jesuit Father Mulledy and Philadelphia Bishop Kendrick for consideration for the Coadjutor of the New York Diocese, then under the care of the ailing Bishop, John DuBois. On November 3rd, notification of the selection of Hughes to this difficult assignment arrived in the United States.[46] Shortly after receipt of the Pope's decision, Hughes advised his flock of the pending change, and they were deeply saddened at the news of the loss of their beloved pastor. For over 10 years, Hughes had labored diligently in building up and ministering to a parish. He had simultaneously built respect for his people and Church in the non-Catholic community, who now overwhelmed him with invitations for dinners, awards and just the chance to wish him well in his new work. The challenges of the New York diocese were still, for the moment, unfocused and in the future. For one thing, Hughes was clearly not the primary choice of Bishop Dubois. The New York nativist scene was as raw and vitriol filled as any Hughes had experienced up to this point in his career, and was destined to become more so with the immigration explosion of the desperately poor masses of Irish Catholics fleeing famine in Ireland. There were to be continued battles in print, with Hughes facing a new coterie of anti-Catholic and anti-immigrant propagandists with names like James Gordan Bennett and George Templeton Strong. These and numerous other aspects of what was to unfold in the Hughes epoch in New York was to have a greater and more far reaching impact on the Catholic Church in the United States than anyone could have possibly imagined in November, 1837. For the moment, the young crusading hero of Catholicism could take solace in the letter he received from Bishop DuBois dated November 6th:

My Dear Friend:

Your favor of the 31st Ultimo, which is the only information (official) I received of your nomination by the Holy See to the coadjutorship of New York, afford me much consolation, in the hope that you will find in it, as I do, an expression of the divine will. One part of your letter only created in me a painful sensation: I allude to the apprehension of a contingent disunion which might take place between the bishop and the coadjutor. You surely could not suppose a moment that I would encroach upon the rights and privileges attached to that sacred office, and I have too great an opinion of your merit and affection for me to suppose that you would encroach upon mine. As a counsel, I shall more readily yield to your wishes, as your resolutions will pave the way to the course which you will have to pursue hereafter; but when conscience or experience would demand a dissent of opinion on any subject, this dissent of opinion could not produce a division of hearts or arrest our proceedings. That scandals should have arisen between Bishop Conwell and his coadjutor, who is ex-officio sole administrator of the diocese, is no wonder, with a man of the bishop's disposition, but I am neither reduced to the nullity of Bishop Conwell – a circumstance rather painful to human pride – nor would I be disposed to struggle for the mastery if I had been placed in the situation; I would have considered this nullity a warning from the divine goodness that henceforth all my time must be exclusively devoted to my preparation for death; but as it is, you may be sure that I will always be happy to act in concert with you.

Whilst you are in Baltimore, you have an opportunity to extract from the canonical books the rights and privileges attached to the coadjutorship, you will oblige me to take a copy of the same, and you may he assured that I am more disposed to extend rather than to restrain them.

May almighty God guide you, for his greater honor and glory; and be assured that, as I already proved to you, you have a sincere and devoted friend in

> Your humble servant,
> + John,
> *Bishop of New York*[48]

At the core of the American Catholic Church lay a problem with respect to nationalities. In the early days of American Catholicism, French clergy who had escaped the excesses of the Revolution in France came to dominate the growing number of Irish, who were starting to swell the ranks of the Catholic laity. To the many Irish, having escaped the tyranny of an English master in their own land, resentment at having to be subservient to French masters in a democracy was beyond galling. Only time would tell how long the hands of amity would mutually extend between the French aristocratic DuBois and his former Irish gardener.[49]

Chapter 5

The Fight for Catholic Education

In the reign of Pope Gregory the XVI, John Joseph Hughes was consecrated the Bishop of Basileopolis in *partibus infidelium*, and coadjutor to the bishop of New York. The consecration took place in St Patrick's Cathedral on Mott Street on January 7th, 1838. Hughes's old superior from Mt. St. Mary's, John DuBois, served as consecrator, assisted by Bishop Kendrick of Philadelphia, who had served as coadjutor to Henry Conwell. Also assisting that day was Bishop Fenwick of the Diocese of Boston. In spite of the freezing temperature, all of the windows of the Cathedral had been opened and platforms had been constructed in the cemetery adjacent to the church in order to facilitate a view of the sanctuary from every possible angle by the huge crowd that had assembled to watch the solemnly impressive ceremony. Father John McCloskey, episcopal successor to Hughes as well as the first American member of the College of Cardinals recalled the majesty of that morning with particular emphasis on the person at center stage: "I remember how all eyes were fixed, how all eyes were strained to get a glimpse of their newly consecrated bishop; and as they saw that dignified and manly countenance, as they beheld those features beaming with the light of intellect, bearing already upon them the impress of that force of character which peculiarly marked him throughout his life, his firmness of resolution, that unalterable and unbending will, and yet blending at the same time that great benignity and suavity of expression – when they marked the quiet composure and self-possession of every look and every gesture of his noble gait and demeanor – all hearts were drawn and warmed to him. Every pulse within the vast assembly, both of clergy and of laity, was quickened with a higher sense of courage and hope. Every breast was filled with joy, and, as it were, with a new and younger might."[1] Hughes, forty years old when he commenced his episcopal mission in New York, was well into his middle years by the standards of that time. There was nothing about his physical condition however which would have revealed anything of the sagging and flabbiness which accompanies advancing age. In appearance, Hughes more resembled a man familiar with the inside of a boxing ring than of a priest. A lean and very muscular man, he had long ago parted with any vestige of his Irish birth, and from accent to appearance had transformed himself into being thoroughly American. Gone was the day laborer and gardener, for that individual had become a man of solid cultural background. Gone was the lack of confidence in the ability to communicate both verbally and the written word. He was a man that stood out in a crowd. His brown curling hair had just started to recede, exposing a large forehead and more prominent Roman nose. His blue-grey eyes were capable of either brimming with loving charity, or, depending on the circumstances and company, a cold and prickly anger. He was self-possessed and confident in a manner which could be perceived by others as intimidating. In all instances, he advanced himself in a self-assuring manner. In stark contrast to the man Hughes had come to assist, John DuBois had come to New York in 1826 as an unpopular person before he even took up his duties as bishop. He was viewed as the usurper of the man who the small, Catholic population of the city, mostly Irish, had wanted to see become bishop, Vicar General of the Diocese, John Power.

It was said of DuBois that he possessed a strange sense of ethnicity in that his appeals to a diocese composed mostly of Irish Catholics, who were ardent supporters of Power, focused on trying to ascribe the nationality of St. Patrick to France. "Is St. Patrick less the patron and protector of Ireland for having been born in Gaul?"[2] Aside from DuBois's faulty sense of geography concerning the birthplace of St. Patrick, he attempted to appeal to his flock not from the standpoint of specific ethnic identity, but rather, from the standpoint of being Catholic. "We are all Catholics. Are not all distinctions of birth and country lost in this common profession?"[3] DuBois was maligned for being a poor preacher, his English halting and so poor that people by the score literally got up at Mass and left during his sermons. DuBois however was as determined as he was tough, and he buckled down to administering a diocese filled with nothing but quarrelsome clergy and laity. Far from the idyllic forest setting around Emmitsburg, people in New York automatically disliked DuBois before they even met him. In 1828, he undertook an extensive visitation of the diocese. In exploring around the area where the Erie Canal was under construction, he literally found hundreds of Irish Catholics who were without a priest. He promised to try and find them one, but to no avail. In 1829, he set out to undertake a begging tour of the Catholic Churches in Europe. DuBois had a sincere concern and worry for the Catholic Church in America; he was motivated by an obsession to tend to the needs of an infant Church. He was determined to build a seminary in the diocese along the same lines as the Mt. Saint Mary's facility in Emmitsburg. One of his principle objectives was to try and tap into the sources for priests willing to be missionaries in America. In each of the countries where efforts may have proven fruitful, DuBois ran up against a stone wall. Europe at the time of his visit was in a tumultuous state. France was wracked by Revolution and Ireland was too destitute to be of much help to anyone. Though he had been granted a free hand with respect to his solicitations, he returned home to New York with the miserable sum of $3,000.00. The ongoing skirmishes with Power all but rendered the work of DuBois extremely tense at best. Complaints going back to Rome included recriminations against the aging bishop for his lack of financial acumen, a condition that had afflicted him during his days in Emmitsburg. Writing to Father Paul Cullen of the Irish College in Rome, Power said that "our aged bishop" has sunk the parish into debt."[4] In addition to the pesky presence of Power, there was the ill-tempered and equally disagreeable Thomas Levins, who continuously proved to be the greatest thorn in the side of DuBois. Levins had little if any respect for Dubois, as he felt he was too often engaged in capricious and idealistic programs that came to nothing. DuBois at one point suspended Levins because the hostility had become so open and so vitriolic, Dubois had no alternative in dealing with a man who had obviously felt no reservations about crossing the line of decency and civility. As to DuBois's ambitious plan to create another Mt. St. Mary's in Emmitsburg, the college he started building up the Hudson in Nyack, New York had been under construction for some years. In 1835, the buildings burned to the ground and were uninsured. Toward the end of the 1830s, DuBois himself came to realize that he was in need of help in the running of his toxic diocese. He needed the help of the Irish, a consideration which DuBois had hoped to never have given serious consideration to, but with the reality of existing animosities, became a necessity. In viewing a possible assistant, DuBois immediately settled on Philadelphia's Kendrick, a man who was enough of a gentleman to mitigate the harsh battering that DuBois was so accustomed to receiving. Kendrick however was not an enthusiastic prospect. He did not know DuBois well and was reluctant to replicate a similar situation to the one he was currently suffering under Henry Conwell. He resisted DuBois's entreaties. The matter was settled in 1837, when Rome decided that instead of Kendrick, Hughes would be sent to New York. There is no doubt that DuBois viewed Hughes as one of his children of the "wilderness," having put him on the road to the holy Catholic priesthood and lifelong service to God. Hughes however was a more unforgiving person than DuBois ever knew. For Hughes, affections of friendship with DuBois was a very one-sided affair, one-sided as far as DuBois was concerned. Hughes never felt the warmth of sonship so effusively expressed by DuBois. To Hughes, he would always remember the relationship with DuBois as "a regular contract between us, in which neither was required to acknowledge any obligation to the other."[5] For the moment, past perceived hurts could be held aside. New York was a veritable cauldron, and her newest bishop was about to exponentially increase the temperature of the pot.

I

The population of the United States was steadily growing. In New York City alone, the population was multiplying at about five times the national rate. The line of settlement was moving further north, and by the late 1830s had reached Fourteenth Street. A physical description of the Diocese of New York at the time of the arrival of John Hughes would have included a geographic area encompassing not only all of the State of New York, but approximately half of the State of New Jersey. Within this huge and unwieldy territory, there were a total of twenty-two Catholic Churches, many of which were in acute financial difficulty. Of the twenty-two Churches, ten had been established since 1837. The total regional population at the time was 2,700,000, of which there were approximately 220,000 Roman Catholics. The Catholic population was served by a total of forty priests. Only one religious order was represented in the New York Diocese and they were the Emmitsburg Sisters of Charity. There were a total of seven Catholic schools, all located in New York City and four orphanage asylums, of which two were located in New York City. This made up the total of Catholic religious, educational and charitable institutions of the time.[6] DuBois's health had never been robust, and even though he had swung a pick and had dug many a spade during his mission days, he started suffering a series of debilitating strokes, the first of which occurred about two weeks after the arrival of his coadjutor. Throughout the next year, the continued decline of DuBois's health rendered him unfit to continue the discharge of his ministry. In August of 1839, Hughes was name Apostolic Administrator, in effect being given responsibility for the day to day operations of the diocese. In a letter to his St. Joseph's benefactor, Mr. M.A. Frenaye, Hughes wrote in February of 1838 that "Bishop Dubois does not recover very fast this time as the first. His appetite is not so good, and his spirits have sunk. He insists on seeing every one that comes to inquire for him, and the consequence is that toward the evening of every day he is extremely feeble, both in body and mind."[7] As in the past, controversy was never far from Hughes, and just as anticipated, its ugly head was not long in raising itself. DuBois, in spite of past assurances, had been reluctant to give up the reigns. While DuBois's body and mind may have been failing him, he had not been prepared to admit that the diocese, in the waning days of his episcopacy, was cruising straight toward disaster. Not having to further wait on the infirmities of the bishop for crisis to be precipitated, a group of clergy along with some of the laity were already planning a test of the "new comer" to see who was really in charge. The fray began when a Sunday school teacher, who had been hired by DuBois, was fired from his position by Thomas Levins, the priest who had been once suspended by DuBois for gross insubordination. The victim of the firing refused to accept his fate, and so Levins decided to call in the law to physically remove the teacher from the premises. On February 10th, 1839, a constable showed up at a Sunday school session and ejected the fired teacher. Hughes was apoplectic. Calling to mind the Hogan like tactics employed in Philadelphia, Hughes was rallied to swift and decisive action against the Sunday school conspirators. At Mass the following Sunday, Hughes, from the pulpit, demanded an abject apology from the trustees. Levins in the meanwhile had been distributing circulars at all of the Masses that day outlining the position of the trustees. At first, none of the participants cared what the reaction of Hughes would be, no doubt comfortable in their belief that they were facing a weak proxy of DuBois. They had all fatally miscalculated. On Sunday, February 24th, Hughes unleashed a counter attack. In a firmly worded pastoral letter, while Hughes acknowledged the prerogatives of the trustees with respect to the temporal affairs of the church, he stated that if they were adamant in exercising the autonomous use of this right, the cathedral would be interdicted and the clergy removed. Further, Hughes said that anyone wishing to discuss the matter with him could do so at as meeting to be held that afternoon in the church hall. Several hundred parishioners attended the meeting, and Hughes, at his absolute best, threw down the gauntlet. As his audience was primarily Irish, Hughes wasted no time alluding to the trustees as destroyers of their beloved Catholic Faith, men of the same ilk as those who pursued the Catholic priest on the lonely mountain ranges and hedges of Ireland in the days of the accursed penal laws. Hughes literally browbeat the audience into acceptance of a series of resolutions whereby they agreed to recognize the judgement of the bishop in matters of the exercise of his official power, no matter what the trustees might say. The audience, stunned at the unaccustomed show of raw ecclesiastic power, accepted the resolutions by acclamation. When the actual resolutions were subsequently printed, some of the trustees resigned and Levins was silenced. This was a pattern that Hughes was to vigorously and aggressively employ as time passed. More and more he sidestepped trustee laws. He would very effectively utilize this tactic in dealing with the trustees of the numerous, financially strapped parishes.

From now on, financial assistance was predicated on the ability of Hughes to retain complete control, leaving the lay boards essentially as figureheads. While trustees would continue to have a limited say in financial matters, Hughes essentially stripped them of any power whatsoever as regards clergy issues or church property. In the healthier parishes, Hughes, by mere force of his personality, started to squeeze the influence of trustees dry. Hughes was demonstrating to his flock that he would stop at nothing in his efforts to break the grip of Trusteeism in New York, and for the first time, the Faithful realized that they were dealing with a serious religious leader. Control of Church property in the hands of one man was not lost on Protestants, who watched warily as Hughes slowly but confidently began the process of dismantling the ruling lay element of the New York Church. The lessons of Philadelphia had taught Hughes well, for never again would the reigns of Church power be held by non-clergy. The invocation of moral authority was a weapon to be pointed by Hughes with great accuracy over the next two and one half decades at enemies both inside as well as outside of the Church.[8]

In October of 1839, Hughes set sail on the packet ship Louis Phillippe bound for Le Havre, France. The object of his European mission was to obtain assistance in priests and money for the New York Diocese. Hughes would visit Paris, Vienna, Dublin and Rome, where he would confer with the Holy Father, both freely expressing the needs of and requesting help for his diocese. He would also solicit aid from the Leopoldine Society, which gave a very generous donation toward the college and seminary he was intending to establish. With respect to the great needs of his people, Hughes wrote to the society that "The zeal of the Catholic emigrants springs, as has been already remarked, from their ardent desire to have a priest; and the consequence, which is unforeseen and unavoidable in their circumstances, is that the churches are generally in *debt*. The people contribute liberally according to their means, but it must be remembered that they are only poor emigrants, just commencing in a new country, and struggling to supply the first great want of their condition, viz,. the want of religion."[9] Writing to Father Felix Varela, Hughes expressed both gratitude and optimism for things to come: "I have been as successful in the object of my visit to Europe as I could have anticipated. The rest must be with ourselves. Since I left you I have not ceased to labor for the object which is so important for the interest of religion in New York, and which is so near to my heart."[10]

II

Upon his return from Europe, Hughes, having successfully completed the pacification of troublesome trustees, directed his immense energy into the advancement of Catholic education. His dream of a college and seminary was coming to fruition, and he directed the movement of the diocesan seminary than located in LaFargerville to the Fordham section of the Bronx. It was on the site of the Rose Hill estate, purchased for a sum of $30,000.00, that St. John's College officially opened in 1841. The first president of the college was the Reverend Father John McCloskey. St. John's College was to evolve into one of the most esteemed institutions of Catholic higher learning, Fordham University. On a more basic level concerning education, in Hughes's absence, his flock had been hard at war in laying out the battleground for what was to become for John Hughes one of his most far reaching and controversial of fights, that is, the attempt to procure public tax money for the purpose of funding Catholic education. If the Breckinridge encounters represented an attempt to bring the Catholic religion out of intellectual obscurity into the mainstream of accepted American religious practice, the school controversy was an attempt to inject Catholicism into the very heart of the Protestant nativist power structure of New York City. The stakes for Hughes in this fight were far greater in that the prize was the right of Roman Catholicism to not only establish its right to exist but to unabashedly and unapologetically makes its needs known.

Starting in 1839, the American Bible Society aggressively opened a campaign to insure that the Bible be placed in every schoolroom in the United States. In a predominantly Protestant nation, there was no disagreement among the various denominations of Protestantism as to the soundness of this proposal. To most Protestants, the belief that any education worthy of it name had as its underpinning the Bible. In this respect, Horace Mann, the father of American public school education said that "Our system earnestly inculcates all Christian morals. It welcomes the religion of the Bible; and in receiving the Bible, it allows it to do what is allowed by no other system – to speak for itself."[11] The version of the Bible universally accepted by all of the Protestant denominations was the King James Version. By its use, Protestants understood that there would be nothing either in favor of or prejudicial against one particular sect. The King James Version was therefore considered to be non-sectarian. The King James Bible possessed assumptions about Christianity universally held by all Protestants, and therefore was used as the basis for public education. The word "sectarian" was soon to take on a different meaning. As the school funding controversy started heating up, sectarian would become synonymous with "Catholic."[12] Within the common schools of New York City, and elsewhere, daily scripture readings from the Kings James Version, along with prayers, songs and general religious instruction at odds with Catholic belief became the norm. Ant-Catholic sentiment was freely expressed throughout the program of religious instruction, with generous reference to deceitful Catholics, vile popery, murderous inquisitions, Church corruption, conniving Jesuits and the Pope as the "Whore of Babylon."[13] In the face of this scurrilous onslaught against Catholic school children, some parishes fought back by establishing their own Catholic-centered schools. By 1840, approximately 5,000 children were attending eight such schools operating in the diocese. Another 12,000 Catholic children either attended no school or were forced to attend the common schools.[14] While Hughes was in Europe, an Albany priest, the Reverend Father Schneller, having been in conversation with several members of the New York State Legislature, became somehow impressed with the idea that Catholics would be able to receive a portion of the public monies available from the school fund if they applied for it. The newly elected Whig Governor of New York, William Seward, was sympathetic to the plight of children, particularly immigrant children with respect to their being able to receive instruction from teachers who not only spoke their own language, but who shared the same religious beliefs as well. Seward recommended legislation to this effect: "The children of foreigners, found in great numbers in our populous cities and towns, and in the vicinity of our public works, are too often deprived of the advantages of our system of public education, in consequence of prejudice arising from differ-ences of language or religion. It ought never to be forgotten that the public welfare is as deeply concerned in their education as that of our own children. I do not hesitate, therefore, to recommend the establishment of schools in which they may be instructed by teachers speaking the same language with themselves and professing the same faith."[15] With this political opening, a Catholic Association was formed in the city for the purpose of organizing and preparing for a formal submission to the appropriate author- ities to establish the claim for funds. Meetings were organ- ized and held over a period of several months. Finally, the following petition was submitted to the Board of Assistant Alderman:

> "The Petition of the Catholics of New York respect- fully represents: That your petitioners yield to no class in their performance of, and disposition to perform all of the duties of citizens they bear, and are willing to bear, their portion of every common burden; and feel themselves entitled to a participa- tion in every common benefit. This participation, they regret to say, has been denied them for years back, in reference to Common School Education in the city of New York, except on conditions with which their conscience, and, as they believe their duty to God, did not, and do not leave them at liberty to comply."[16]

The Public School Society provided the stock reply, that is, any allowance of public monies for the purpose of funding Catholic education would result in the replacement of public schools, a statement that was as patently absurd as it was bigoted. The petition was denied. Hughes wasted no time in emasculating the Public School Society's position. He roundly condemned it as a system that actively promoted the degra- dation of Catholic school children. Hughes than forwarded to the Society another petition demanding that Catholics be given a portion of state monies and was again rebuffed. The second reply of refusal came not only from the Public School Society but from the Methodist Church, which seized on the opportunity to launch an all out attack against the Catholic Church, focusing of course on the stock Protestant innuendo about Catholics in their "unqualified" submission to the Pope as well as being murderers of heretics and idolaters. Rather than attempt to have a discussion of the proposal on its merits, the atmosphere was once again poisoned by the charges of Catholic infamy and malfeasance. With the increasing numbers of poor Irish immigrants making their way into places like New York, the Methodist attack against Catholicism found new focus in that the Irish were depicted not only as minions of the Pope, but as being shiftless and drunkards. More and more, the Irish were depicted in news illustrations with ape-like features, and the nativist Protestant establishment asserted that the Irish could never be assimilated into the institutions of democracy, especially because of their coarse and crude pedigree. What had prompted so violent a reaction to what many Catholics believed to be merely a matter of religious equality? Were not Roman Catholics as taxpayers entitled to be the beneficiaries of taxpayer monies in the same manner any other citizen was? Was not the Roman Catholic parent entitled to also provide for the education of his child in a manner reflective of the religious and spiritual values of that parent? At a mass meeting held in the school-house attached to St. Patrick's Church on July 20th, 1840, Hughes asked the question: "It is the sacred right of every man to educate his own children, and when these are the consequences that follow this system of common school education, is it just to tax a man for its support, while its tendency is to draw away the mind of his child from the religion which he professed and which he desired to teach him?"[17] The real crux of the issue with respect to aid to Catholic schools touched on more than just simple moral justice, for it represented a threat to one of the basic tenets of American democracy, the separation of church and state. While many advocates of the petition for the request of funds believed with all sincerity that this was not a political question, a slanderous article appearing in the publication the *Truth Teller* sought to impute to petition supporters sinister and unworthy objectives, "and were preparing to press upon the Corporation of the city a demand which, if complied with, would be a palpable violation of the constitution of the State, and the equality of rights which it secured for all citizens."[18] To the extremist elements within Protestant nativist ranks, this was tantamount to a declaration of war. Again, Hughes was finding in this arena yet another avenue for his logical and effective oratory. Questioning the very absurdity of the "sectarian" aspect of the School Society's position, Hughes, speaking in the basement of St. James Church on the evening of July 27th, 1840, with typical, biting sarcasm, shredded the exclusion of Catholics from receipt of educational aid by using the image of a common man thrashing out the faulty logic of the School Society: "But now, to show them that that the exclusion of sectarianism was impossible – did not those directors each belong to some sect? He came to this point that that they either belonged to some sect or acted on the principles of deism; and though this system had now no name under a religious head, it was either deism or sectarianism. If it was said that is was not sectarianism, he wanted to know what was Christianity, for if they excluded all sects, they excluded all Christianity. Where are the Christians? Take away Catholics, and Baptists, and Methodists, and Presbyterians and some others – and they were all sects – take away all the sects and they had no more Christianity in the land. Nor could they exclude sectarianism? And if they did, what remained but deism? There was no alternative. It was as plain as that two and two are four. And did they suppose that this community which belonged to one or the other sect would subscribe to a system which in essence was anti-Christian? Exclude sectarianism! And in a country, too, which prides itself on Christianity!"[19]

The battle with respect to school funding for Catholics was taking on dimensions of the Breckinridge conflict, in that the passions and emotions of the parties involved found outlets both in the press as well as the great halls of public debate. In an attack against funding for Catholic Schools that appeared in the *Evening Post* in September of 1840 by a person signing their letter as an "Irish Catholic," Hughes responded to the slanderous accusations made against Catholics with respect to the funding issue, as well the charge that Hughes was himself the willing dupe of the Whigs: "Mr. Editor: Your correspondent who signs himself "An Irish Catholic," and dedicates his homily to me by name, must be a very inconsistent man. He must know that thousands of the children of poor Catholic parents are growing up without education, simply because the law is

interpreted and administered under the Public School
Society, which requires a violation of their rights of conscience. The number of children may be from nine to twelve
thousand. Of these the Catholics, of bearing a double
taxation, educate four or five thousand; a few hundred have
attended the Public Schools; and the rest may be considered
as receiving only such education as is afforded in the streets
of New York."[20] Hughes, as anyone in his position would
justifiably believe, that any Irish Catholic, given the history
of that group in Ireland, would "see in this state of things
quite enough to excite my personal solicitude for the spiritual and moral condition of the people committed to my
charge."[21] As to the charge of being a puppet whose strings
were being pulled by Whig political interest, Hughes replied
that "When I returned to this city, I found Catholics broken
up and divided, thanks to the interference of such men as
your correspondent. Now, happily, that question has been
relieved of the dead weight of politicians of either side, they
are united... We meet to understand the injuries which we
are compelled to suffer, and to seek for their removal.
Among the sufferers are men of both parties – and our object
is to seek justice from just and upright men, who will
comprehend our grievances without distinction of party."[22]

After several months of Church organizing meetings and
petitions, the Board of Alderman of New York City convened
in a special session on October 29th, 1840 to consider the
petition of Catholics with respect to receiving their share of
monies from the Common School Fund. In stern opposition
to this petition were the Public School Society and the
Societies of the Methodist Episcopal Church. In attendance
by invitation of the Board of Alderman was the Board of
Assistant Alderman, the body to whom the original petition
had been forwarded. Huge public interest had attached to
this discussion given the packed Council Chamber and
overflow crowds jammed into the corridors. The participants
of the proceedings made their way into the room with great
difficulty, struggling to get inside even with the assistance of
a staunch body of police officers. When the entrants finally
made their way to their respective places and events settled,
the meeting opened with the petitioners to be heard in the

order in which their petitions and replies had been received. First would be the Catholics, followed by the Public School Society to be followed by the Societies of the Methodist Episcopal Church. The representatives of these group were respectively: Right Reverend Bishop Hughes and the very Reverend Dr. John Power, Thomas O'Connor, Esq., Francis Cooper, Esq., Dr. Hugh Sweeney, James McKeon, Esq. and James Kelly, Esq. for the Catholic side; Theodore Sedgwick, Esq. and Hiram Ketchum, Esq. for the School Society and the Reverends Dr. Bangs, Dr. Bond and Mr. George Peck for the Methodists. Mr. John Paulding, the reader of the Board, formally opened the session with a reading of the Catholic petition and all the responses against it. As Hughes was the first speaker, he once again was center stage on a major platform to defend and advance the cause of his Church. Hughes commenced his remarks by separating issues from people: "I am sorry therefore that the Public School Society should have been pleased to refer to the language of our document as though imputation dishonorable to them personally as gentlemen. We speak of their system apart from themselves; and we speak of it with that freedom which it is the right of American citizens to speak of the public actions and proceedings of public men; but again will I repeat, that in no instance to my knowledge has there been imputed to those gentlemen one solitary motive, one single purpose unworthy of their high standing and their reputable character."[23] Saddened by the negative arguments advanced by those who chose to reject the approval of monies for Catholic schools, Hughes lamented that "I am exceedingly sorry that the gentlemen who drew up the remonstrance had not more confidence in the power of their own religious principle than to suppose that it would be necessary to contend violently for what they call "spoils." We have submitted to be deprived of them for years, and we have not manifested such a disposition; and I am surprised that they who understand so much of the power of religion should attach so much value to the little money which is to be distributed as to suppose that it would set Christians – professing Christians – together by the ears in its distribution."[24] In calling to mind the past, Hughes defiantly challenged his opponents to answer the question as to whether the future generation of Catholics are or should be persecuted and denied on the basis of ancient excesses, avowing the intentions of the present generation of Catholics to sincerely avoid perpetuating memory of the historically painful experiences between Catholics and Protestants: "Did not the Roman Catholics know, that they addressed many of their fellow-citizens who could not recur to the memoirs of their ancestors without being reminded of the revocation of the Edict of Nantz – the massacre of St. Bartholemew's day, the fires of Smithfield. What is that to us? Are we the people who took part in that, or the crusade against the Waldenses? We would willingly cover these scenes with the mantle of charity. They had better not make the attempt for their mantle is too narrow and hope that Our Roman Catholic fellow-citizens will in future avoid whatever has a tendency to revive the painful remembrance."[25]

Dr. Bond, Mr. Ketchum, Mr. Sedgwick, Dr. Spring and a host of others made both vigorous and acrimonious replies to the arguments put forth by Bishop Hughes. In reply to these persons, Bishop Hughes, on the second day of the proceedings, remonstrated that "I am not accustomed to the niceties of legislation or the manner of interpreting statutes or acts by the Legislature; but to sum up the whole of the two eloquent addresses made by the gentlemen who have just spoken, they amount to this: that either the consciences of the Catholics must be crushed and their objections resisted, or the Public School System must be destroyed. That is the pith of both their observations."[26]

Governor William Seward was sympathetic to the Catholic position and in April of 1841, his Secretary of State, John C. Spencer, himself an ex-offcio superintendent of the public schools, drafted and submitted a report to the state senate on the issue. The paper unreservedly supported the legitimacy of the right of Catholics to be the recipients of public monies for their schools. Spencer further went on to state how contentions of the "sectarian" nature of Catholic education were specious, and all forms of instruction were, in reality, sectarian in one form or another. Spencer recommended that the New York Public School Society be dissolved and replaced by a board of commissioners, who would be charged with all matters connected to instruction. As far as religious instruction was concerned, these matters would be left to the trustees of the individual schools. As expected, the legislature stalled with respect to the Spencer recommendations. As it became more and more evident that neither Democratic nor Whig candidates for election were prepared to take a stand on the issue, Hughes initiated a radical departure from the Catholic Church's previous position of timidity concerning Catholic issues. He boldly endorsed a slate of political candidates for the New York State legislature, who were specifically committed to the passage of the reforms needed to procure tax money for Catholic education. Hughes was resorting to the power of the ballot box to make his point, and in a manner characteristic of parish priests leading their disciplined flocks to vote for Daniel O'Connell in the Clare by Election of 1828, he was demonstrating the ability to organize his people to press for the recognition of their rights through the franchise. It was a serious gamble. Hughes believed that there was no other course to take: "I have found myself imperatively called upon to take the position which I have assumed for the protection of the religious rights of those entrusted to my charge."[27] On October 25th, 1841, in a meeting held at Carrol Hall, an impassioned Hughes warned his fellow Catholics of the inherent dangers of their cause being lost for failure to give their support to anyone other than those willing to support the new school and system, and ultimately, financial aid for Catholic schools."Under the free and happy institutions of our country, the power to redress grievances and remedy abuses has not an abstract existence. It is something practical – something that comes home to every individual; and if any set of men entrusted with authority should molest and injure others by the evil exercise of their power, the oppressed have, in time, their turn also, when they can vindicate their rights and divest their oppressors of the authority of which they had abused."[28] A line in American political life was about to be crossed. Since the inception of the Republic, the divide between governance and the practice of religion had become more and more separated. The mere suggestion of a "Catholic vote" in support of specific issues was sufficient to raise the ire and irrational fears of Protestants. On October 29th, one week before the election, Catholics once again assembled at Carroll Hall. An independent ticket of candidates for the New York State senate and assembly, already before the public and understood to have refused to sign the pledge required by the School Society with respect to electing no candidate favoring support of tax money for Catholic education, was proposed and accepted. The "Carroll Hall" candidates were acclaimed by a thunderous ovation. Hughes rose to address the group: "I am not acquainted with any of these individuals; but they have been selected by gentlemen as much interested in this question as I am; and now, if you are unanimously determined to convince this community that you are in earnest – that you sincerely feel there is a bona fide grievance of which you complain, you will support candidates thus offered for your choice; because if you do not, you have no alternative left but that of voting for the enemies of your rights... You have often voted for others and they did not vote for you, but now you are determined to uphold with your own votes your own rights."[29] The statement made by Hughes was unprecedented in that a Roman Catholic Bishop was urging his people to act as a block, as a unit with respect to an important issue based on deeply held religious beliefs. It was totally hypocritical to label as "sectarian" bias Catholic religious beliefs with respect to education, even though every single sect of Protestantism was individually possessed of its own sectarian peculiarities. Protestants were horrified at such a raw display of political power, but for Hughes, he was merely exercising one of the very democratic rights that Protestant nativists so nobly cherished and enshrined with respect to American democracy: the right to vote. Hughes, his voice rising in emotion, yet steady and exact in every word asked of his supporters: "Will you then stand by the rights of your offspring, who have so long suffered under the operation of this injurious system? Will you adhere to the nomination made? Will you be united? Will you let all men see that you are worthy sons of the nation to which you belong? Will you prove yourselves worthy of friends....? Will none of you flinch?"[30]

The Catholic editor of the *New York Herald*, James Gordon Bennett, a man whom Hughes was to cross swords with on many issues even though they were co-religionists, excoriated Hughes for the political tactics used in attempting to organize Catholics into a distinct political party, which could be bartered to the Whigs or Locofocos[31] at the wave of his crozier. Bennett fulminated in the *Herald* how "the whole thing from beginning to end is only a preposterous insult to the common sense of an intelligent community. To all minds of intelligence, it will, after the election is over, reduce Bishop Hughes to the lowest state of degradation and contempt. He has shown himself to be utterly deficient in honesty or in common sense. If he meant seriously, in a protestant country, to succeed in his project, he took the very method that would forever put a barrier between his Church and the claim on the School Fund. One of the first principles of American freedom is to keep distinct the institutions of the Church and State. No element of liberty is more deeply imbued in the American mind than this is. How, then, in such a happy, and free, and positive condition of public opinion, could bishop Hughes expect that if the Church of Rome had a favor to ask of a protestant country, the best method to acquire it was to trample this holy principle under foot, and organize the Church into a political Club."[32]

Gordon's apologetics for the nativist establishment did not prevent the Hughes slate from going forward in the election and winning a great tactical victory. The candidates received enough protest votes to end any further discussion with respect to providing public funds for aiding any school. At the next session of the state legislature, the once pro Protestant Public School Society was, in effect, no longer regarded as the governing body of the New York City common schools. Going forward, no public monies would be allocated to any religious school, and a new non-sectarian Board of Education was created to both oversee and administer the provisions of the new law. In addition to moral vindication for Hughes, New York in effect became the first of the original thirteen American states to expressly prohibit the teaching of any kind of religious doctrine in the public schools.

In the aftermath of the school decision, St. Patrick's, the Cathedral Church of the New York Diocese located on Prince Street between Mott and Mulberry Streets and Bishop Hughes's episcopal residence on Mulberry Street were attacked by a nativist mob. In the course of the rampage, windows and furniture were damaged, and while it was Hughes's good fortune to not be at home when the attack took place, it did not prevent the Episcopalian activist and lawyer, George Templeton Strong, from enthusiastically recoding the following entry in his diary dated the 13th of April, 1842: "We had some hard fighting yesterday in the Bloody Sixth, and a no-popery riot last night, including a vigorous attack on the Roman Catholic Cathedral with bricks and bats and howls, and a hostile demonstration on Hughes's episcopal palace, terminating in broken windows and damaged furniture. Also, the Spartan Band got into the Sixth Ward Hotel, as the no-popery rioters of old did in 'the Maypole,' and 'made a noise and broke things' in great style. Well, this is the beginning of the end, the first fruits of that very abominable tree – the School Bill."[33]

While Protestant trustees of their own schools could and would continue to remain influential with respect to how religion was taught in their own schools, "Catholic" education would never again be denied to Catholic children for want of their own schools. The display of such awesome political power was unnerving to the nativist population. Hughes set about creating his own school system. It was an omen of things to come. On the heels of the school controversy, a great floodgate was crumbling across the Atlantic. Within a few short years, places like New York would start receiving the first casualties of the deadly potato famine that was ravaging Ireland. The new immigrants were not only desperately impoverished but Catholic, and their overpowering numbers seeking relief from starvation and destitution would greatly expand the limits of nativist intolerance. Into this vacuum would again step John Hughes, prepared as always to employ the full essence of his being in the fight to raise and lift the weak and most vulnerable, in this instance, his own countrymen. John Hughes would take the battered, human refuse of famine-ridden Ireland and start building a Faith community not only devoted to the Church, but to their newly adopted land. In refashioning the Catholic Church as one which catered to the spiritual and material needs of Irish immigrants, Hughes would simultaneously start laying the ground work for the emergence of a larger, robust and more militant American Catholicism.

Chapter 6

Building and Defending the Immigrant Church

The conversion from grain to cattle by Irish landlords in the years following the end of the Napoleonic wars was to have far reaching and catastrophic effects on the population. The conversion prompted steep increases in the rents paid by peasant farmers, most of whom were Catholic. These measures resulted in dire economic hardship and massive increases in the number people being evicted from the land. In the period from 1821 until 1842, the population of Ireland increased from 6.8 to nearly 8.2 million.[1] The greatest population increase of the country during this period was among persons who owned no land and who were allowed access to a landlord's holding only for the purpose of harvesting crops. Partible inheritance,[2] early marriage and high birth rates increased immigration to the United States from 665,000 to 1.3 million in the period between 1831 and 1841.[3]

For those who remained at home during this critical period, conditions worsened. As land became scarce and population dramatically increased, the people began relying more and more on the potato for daily sustenance. Introduced into Irish agriculture around 1590, the potato root grew with remarkable ease in Irish soil. The potato fast became the staple of survival for the Irish people, with the average male consuming upwards of fourteen pounds per day. The planting of potatoes was easily accomplished through the setting of seed potatoes into spade-dug ridges covered over with earth. This process came to be of increasingly greater importance to the average Irish farmer, because forced to spend most of his time in the cultivation of a landlord's fields, he had less time available to cultivate food for his own family. With the potato, even the smallest plots of land could sustain large families. Typically, a portion of the crop went toward feeding livestock. Anything else produced by the farm such as butter, bacon, poultry or eggs was sold for whatever money could be made.

The role of the Irish potato was prominent in the ticking population time bomb. The explosion occurred in 1845, when the first of a series of catastrophic crop failures resulting from fungus wreaked devastating famine on Ireland. "An Gorta Mor," or Great Hunger, as it was to be known through successive generations was, for the Irish people, its Holocaust. The net result was a loss in Irish population between the years of 1845 and 1851 of two million people, who perished through starvation, fever or immigration to the Unites States. The number of immigrating Irish accounted for over half of all immigration to American shores in the decade of the 1840s, and over one third during the 1850s.[4] At first, there was a sympathetic and even proactive response to the plight of the famine sufferers; however, with the passage of time, and as more and more of the "human refuse" of Ireland began pouring through the major ports of entry like New York, the newcomers were reviled and scorned by their white, Protestant nativist predecessors. The newcomers were viewed as an advance guard of the Roman Pope. The United States already had an established history of Protestant nativist hostility toward Catholics; now, the displaced persons represented yet another dimension in the arousal of nativist passions; the newcomers were Irish. Poor, Irish and Catholic were for a long time to be the ignition words for nativist, Protestant antipathy.

When the Irish potato crop turned black, the dynamics of Irish immigration were unalterably changed. The Irish Catholics fleeing the famine were to become the most reviled and unwelcome newcomers that America up to this point in her history had received. Welcome quickly turned to rejection, as the huge numbers of poor, papist sons and daughters of

Erin were perceived as a direct threat to the established social order.

I

For the Catholic poor of Ireland, the cruel divorce of religion from daily life, reinforced by decades of English governmental prohibition, was to play itself out in America. When there is little left, a man will grasp onto whatever remains with greater determination. So it was with the famine era Irishman, divorced from the land of his birth because the alternative was death through starvation. He held on tenaciously to whatever supports remained familiar. Naturally, these thoughts often turned to God, and with the heavy burden of assimilating a strange new culture, religion became a more important handle of survival. For the vast majority of Irish immigrants, once the last view of Ireland beyond the horizon finally disappeared, never again to be seen, the reality of separation made many to cling more strongly to their religious beliefs to whatever degree they existed. For the Irish Catholics, religion and faith was their only link to the past.[5] Still, the material reality of the newly arrived immigrants was a far worse cry from the spiritual.

The Irish Catholics of the famine were the most pitiful lot ever cast down upon the land. Many arrived in sickly conditions. It was a wonder that far more had not perished during the long and physically draining transatlantic voyage. The Irish lacked the education and basic skills needed to even hope to gain a foothold on the lowest step of the dynamically growing and expanding American economy. Completion of the long ocean journey left many in a deteriorated state, unfit for even the most rudimentary agricultural work they may have been accustomed to doing at home in Ireland. Large groups, after being subjected to dockside confidence men and phony rental agents offering to place persons for exorbitant fees into lodging which was non-existent, made their way into the dank and dismal "Irish" slums of New York City. While some did succeed in making it into the interior after gaining a foothold, the vast majority were to be wedded to the despicable nineteenth century hell holes of urban America. Despair, loneliness and alienation fostered by disconnection from familial ties as well as the pressures of living in an ever growing hostile society resulted in excessive drinking and violence. Child mortality was high... 61 percent among those immigrants who arrived in the port of Boston.[6]

Atlantic shippers, though hard pressed, were quite resourceful in assembling a flotilla capable of moving the ongoing cargo of human beings under the most dangerous and unsanitary conditions imaginable. The lack of regulation facilitated tremendous incentive for the vastly inadequate transatlantic passenger trade to put on more and more dilapidated, old and unseaworthy vessels. The resultant conditions bordered on the inhuman. Many vessels rushed into service were converted cargo ships, with no consideration whatsoever for "people" needs. Steerage passage was fraught with a lack of clean water, proper food and sanitary facilities. Sickness, fever and diarrhea were common afflictions. Cramped quarters below decks, especially for persons traveling with infants or very young children, were stifling and oppressive. Women, in many cases, were literally forced to sleep standing up. By voyage's end, people might be rising for the first time, having lain in their own excrement for weeks.[7]

For immigrants who boarded the "coffin ships," the trauma accompanying famine exodus was to leave an enduring legacy. Bitterness was fueled by the reality of having to leave because they no longer possessed a means of subsistence in their own land. Ultimately, it mattered little as to whether their fate was an act of God or part of some sordid evil of man. Those surviving the crossing found they were quickly to find that barely paved, dung covered streets had replaced the gold. In nineteenth century New York, the Irish accounted for 87 percent of the unskilled labor force, and their dismally low percentage of representation in the larger industries such as the building trades and clothing manufacturing was equaled only by their equally dismal living conditions. The principle living area of the poor Irish was the notorious Sixth Ward neighborhood known as the Five Points, which encompassed the corners of Anthony, Orange and Cross Streets, today's Worth, Baxter and Park Streets. Here the Irish generally dwelled in wooden tenement houses, where children played in streets that reeked of a shit-smelling foulness that defied description, and where cattle, pigs, rats and dogs roamed at will. There were no indoor water closets or sewerage disposal. In the adjoining Fourth Ward known as Sweeney's Shambles, another four hundred families were as miserably housed as their Sixth Ward neighbors, while a seven-story tenement housed another fifty families amidst the worst filth, garbage and smells. Trapped in the worst conditions, toiling at the dirtiest and most menial jobs, struggling to retain some semblance of family life, many of the new Irish arrivals slipped into alcoholism, crime and insanity.[8]

II

The early nineteenth century Catholic community of New York was one which much resembled its English counter-part: small, conservative, respectably middle class and quiet. Into this group fit a number of earlier Irish Catholics. With the flood of famine immigrants and the aggressively proac-tive leadership of Hughes, who transformed the Catholic Church in New York into an institution which served the needs of the immigrant poor, the Catholic Church primed itself for a period of robust growth and became the most visible and powerful institution representing the new "downtrodden" of society. Contrary to popular myth about the strong Catholic faith brought to America's shores by Ireland's starving and suffering masses, many of the newcomers were Catholic in name only. After a century and one half of penal servitude, many of the new Irish immi-grants were barely able to make the Sign of the Cross.

In the process of re-churching his immigrant commun-ity, Hughes needed to establish the church as "home." Whether built of wooden planks or bricks, the church building assumed the primacy of place in the ramshackle living areas of the Irish. It was warm and hospitable, a place where one could come in from the bitter cold or pounding rain. It was a meeting place for neighbors, a place to both garner as well as disseminate information. Under the reassuring gaze of saints in stone or the saving visage of the crucified Christ, immigrants prayed in fervent silence, sought solace and asked for deliverance from their inner most trepidations about life in a new and unwelcoming land. Even though Irish Catholics had been forcibly separated from their native religious practices and beliefs through flagrant and callous British misrule, they did attempt to replicate some semblance of their religious experience from home in the religious and church experience of their new environment. They fostered their own special devotions. Piety was revived and developed, with a special emphasis on receipt of the sacraments, especially Baptism and Confirmation. Attendance at Sunday Mass, receiving Holy Communion on a frequent basis, and going to confession at least once a year were all part of the encouraged discipline to be observed with respect to rekindling the Faith. The practice of the "Irish Wake," a custom brought from Ireland, whereby the dead were laid out for days amidst uncontrollable alcohol consumption and ribaldry, was slowly replaced with a more respectful and reverential treatment of death, including the removal of the remains to the church, as well as performing proper Catholic obsequies. Additionally, devotional practice, recitation of the rosary, establishment of religious confraternities and the study of the catechism became the corpus of a well-practiced religion.

Hughes set out to make the Catholic Church more responsive to the material needs of the destitute Irish masses. He embarked on a vigorous program of increasing the number of parishes to make the Church more accessible. Before 1844, there were there were a total of fourteen churches serving the diocese, one of which consisted exclusively of French parishioners and the other two German. By 1844, all the rest exclusively served the Irish. Hughes was greatly dissatisfied that this growth had not kept pace with the ever increasing numbers of immigrants, especially in the years immediately following the failure of the potato crop in Ireland. Nonetheless, Hughes was willing to forgo the appeal for monies to be applied toward the diocesan seminary to be diverted instead to the relief of his decimated homeland and countrymen: "It is better that seminaries should be suspended than that so large a portion of our fellow-beings should be exposed to death by starvation."9 As the result of this collection, Hughes was able to forward the sum of about $14,000.00 to Irish bishops toward famine relief. On the home front, Hughes knew that in order for his Irish outreach to have any chance for success, greater numbers of priests and religious orders were going to be needed. In December of 1845, Hughes once again embarked on a voyage to Europe for the purpose of seeking the assistance of Catholic countries to aid in the tremendous material and spiritual needs of his ever growing but broken and impoverished flock. His visit on this journey was confined to England, Ireland and France. He was obviously most affected by his visit to Ireland, which clearly was the most depressed place of the countries he visited. While at home, he succeeded in procuring the services of the Brothers of Christian Doctrine as well as a community of the Sisters of Mercy, whose principal duties were to visit the sick and protect destitute but virtuous women. Hughes's shopping for religious to help out in New York was not restricted to Europe. He had steadfastly and unrelentingly made overtures to the Jesuits to come and assume operations at St. John's College (later Fordham University) in the Rosehill section of the Bronx. The Sisters of Charity, who had been in the diocese since 1817, and working in both teaching as well as orphanage assignments, were perhaps the most widely known and best thought of religious order in New York. The order's reputation had been secured with the great cholera epidemic of the 1830s, where the sisters faithfully remained at their posts ministering to the needs of the sick and dying in spite of the grievous exposure to themselves. These actions practically made them legendary, even among the most bitter anti-Catholics. So much so was the popularity of the Sisters of Charity, that during the heated school controversy, the only exception to the monies allocated for books went to the order's orphanage school. The public recognition was as great an acknowledgement as could be expected.[10]

Hughes was no glassy-eyed idealist. He explicitly understood that the famine immigrants would face incredible obstacles in their journey to become assimilated into a strange, new and hostile land. He knew that this could only be accomplished if his people were willing to become and be a part of, rather than apart from. While none would ever accuse Hughes of forgetting the land of his birth, he wished the naturalized Irishman of the United States to regard himself an American citizen – not as an exile; he actively deprecated anything that tended to separate the Irish from the mainstream of American people. Consequently, he was no friend to Irish "military societies," "trade societies," "clubs," "institutes" and other similar organizations. Hughes opposed these associations for the Irish because they were apt to inhibit and in many cases prevent the Irish from intercourse with their native-born fellow Americans. Hughes's greatest admonition was to "Never forget your country... love her, defend her when the time comes; but let this love of old Ireland affect you only individually. In your social and political relations, you must become merged in the country of your adoption."[11] Hughes had already demonstrated that the principal means of achieving this objection was education. While Hughes fought against the forces of prejudice and bigotry against his people, he simultaneously extolled the virtues of sobriety, good citizenship and love of America. As the immigrant community began to steady itself and grow in economic strength and confidence, they began to provide the money for the building of churches. Additionally, monies were sent home to help those left behind, as well as gather the latest information. The increasingly significant mail traffic was the lifeline for a people not only separated by a huge body of water, but by a strange culture and its equally strange customs.

Overcoming such apparently tremendous obstacles for the new Irish arrivals would be accomplished by a combination of factors whose origins lay in the famine-ravaged land they had been forced to abandon. Hughes deeply understood the dynamics of Irish social and political life. Because of this understanding, he knew, more than anyone, that since the end of the eighteenth century, with the easing of harsher aspects of the penal laws, Irish Catholics entered into an intense struggle against their English oppressors for the granting of full religious and political liberty. In the Catholic Emancipation and Repeal of the Union with Great Britain movements, it was only natural that Irish Catholics would turn to their Church and clergy for support and leadership. The most potent elixir for English disaster in nineteenth century Ireland was a disestablished Catholic Church, representing the majority of an Irish population who also possessed intensely nationalist aspirations. Irish Catholicism and Irish nationalism were to become united in the same common cause.

As the famine rooted genocide of the Irish nation continued unabated especially in 1846 and 1847, the numbers fleeing the devastation and arriving in New York continued at an unprecedented rate. An estimated one million souls would make the Atlantic crossing between 1846 and 1851. The infrastructure of the Catholic Church was being transformed to accommodate and meet the needs of so many materially and destitute newcomers. No church epitomized the commitment of Hughes to insure that his people did not languish in spiritual poverty more than the Church of St. Brigid. In 1848, Hughes ordered Father Kein to acquire the needed land and to commence building a church at the corner of Avenue B and 8th Street. The church was to be dedicated to St. Brigid, "the virgin Saint of Erin," who heard St. Patrick preach. The cornerstone of the church was laid by Hughes on September 10th, 1848. Huge crowds attended the dedication ceremonies, and the first celebration of Mass took place on Sunday, December 2nd, 1849. The church was designed by the eminent Irish architect, Patrick Keely, at the start of what was to be a career spanning decades and involved in the design of over six hundred Catholic church buildings by the time of his death in 1896. At a time when resources for church buildings were scarce and the cost of architects exorbitant, Keely's designs produced the rare result of being both within budget and on time. St. Brigid's was typical of the Irish churches of the era in that it was strapped for cash. The parish residents were poor and contributed what little they could, while pastors struggled to keep operations afloat. The notion of poor Irish famine immigrants contributing substantial sums of money to construct magnificent church buildings was far from reality, as the Irish immigrant community was living under conditions of dire economic stress.[12] With the steady flow of immigrants as well as the influence and structuring provided by the Catholic Church, the Irish slowly began making the transition into the urban setting and defining themselves as a distinct group.

III

The period from the 1840s until the outbreak of the Civil War was marked by continuous tension and friction between nativists and immigrants. Economic rivalry stemming from competition, even for the most menial of jobs, resulted in both groups living in high degrees of suspicion and social segregation. Democrats were more cosmopolitan in outlook, less sectarian and more concerned with the plight of common people. This fact guaranteed that Irish entry into American political life would be through the Democratic Party. The Whigs were guardians of the more aristocratic outlook, the eighteenth century Puritan tradition of New England and a strong church-state establishment. The notion of the spiritually elect was the underpinning of their moral outlook. Consequently, nativists and Irish immigrants were locked into viewing one another with intense hostility. Many regarded the Irish Catholics as intruders and treated them as inferiors. The Irish deeply resented the flagrant persecution and discrimination experienced at the hands of the Yankees. The Whigs formed what was perceived by the newcomers as the propertied class, and firmly held on to the preservation of Anglo-Protestant tradition. This was intuitively understood by the hordes of poor, Irish Catholics, who in looking at the Whig political establishment saw landlords and their hereditary English enemies. Becoming good Democrats was a painless exercise for the famine Irish immigrants. Nonetheless, Whig leaders like Henry Clay believed that of all foreigners, "none amalgamate themselves so quickly with our people as the natives of the Emerald isle."[13]

The Irish commenced their political apprenticeship in New York as pawns of the Democratic Party machine. Though more widely disposed to Democratic philosophy, the Irish were not initially embraced by their chosen party. Possessed of their own native Irish political acumen, they quickly learned the game of bartering votes in exchange for unskilled jobs, petty licenses and other low cost benefits. These initial scraps were all the newcomers could expect. As the Irish began growing in both numbers and confidence, they started exerting much greater influence in letting the organization know that such scant and ungrateful rewards for loyalty and support would no longer suffice. By the year of 1844, party rolls in New York City showed the Irish were Democrats by a ratio of 95 to 5.

At first the Democratic Party welcomed the Irish as allies, cynically perhaps, but welcoming nonetheless. The Whigs, chafing under their inability to successfully lure Irish votes retaliated with reactionary measures designed to impede the development of Irish participation in the political process. One extraordinarily reactionary proposal was to impose a twenty-one year residency requirement before a person could be naturalized. William Seward was an exception. As Whig governor of New York, he consistently advocated support for the funding of Catholic schools, a measure that was hotly opposed by the legislature and in later years would be the basis for accusations against Hughes that he was an agent for Seward and Seward's political guru, Thurlow Weed. In a pathetic attempt to garner Irish votes for the Whig Presidential candidate, General Winfield Scott, during the Election of 1852, Irishmen were planted in strategic locations during Scott's speaking tours as he unconvincingly gave his assurance to the crowd as to how much he enjoyed hearing the sound of "Irish brogues." The tactic failed miserably, and the simple reality was that the Irish saw nothing of benefit in the Whig program. As Ohio Senator Tom Corwin despondently noted with reference to the election, "We know they *all* {the Irish} voted the other ticket."[14]

From the middle decades of the nineteenth century, Irish votes were being sought out in earnest. In politics, just as religion, the Irish brought to their adopted land communal traits from the old country. As the Irish became reassimilated into Catholicism through contact with Church, parish, benevolent organization and school, they sharpened their inbred political characteristics for the battle against the advantage held by their native American counterparts. The ultimate success and assent of the Irish in places like New York was, to a large measure, attributable to a combination of American urban machine politics with features of nineteenth century rural Ireland. While the Irish did not invent the "machine politics" common to the American political scene of the mid to late 1800s, their communal experience in the homeland, coupled with the disciplined experience of the new Catholicism in their adopted land produced eventual control over American urban politics that was nothing short of remarkable. Hughes wielded his immigrant Church into a force to be reckoned with, and just as Alexis de Tocqueville was struck by the powerful unity between the clergy and the common person during the height of the Repeal and Temperance movements in Ireland, Hughes was prepared to carry out his mission of building and directing a powerful and proactive Catholic Church on the shores of the American Republic: "Roman Catholicism will convert all Pagan nations and all Protestant nations, even England with her proud Parliament. Everyone should know that we have our mission to convert the world, including the inhabitants of the United States, the people of the cities, and the people of the country, the officers of the navy and marines, commander of the Army, the legislatures, the Senate, the Cabinet, the President and all."[15] Much in the character of the Irish immigrant made Hughes's prediction a source of deep concern on the part of native Americans.

In Irish rural areas, decisions were typically made by *clachan* committees. Dissent and lack of conformity was quickly suppressed. This was one possible reason why Irish

Catholics as voters were obedient to the will of their political, and more so, their religious leaders. Having come from a land where oppression and coercion was a normal part of life, the average Irishman had developed a keen and highly intuitive sense of how to skirt around the indignities imposed by English law.

Stuffing ballot boxes or stealing elections was to the Irish less a hanging offence than a mere act of blackguarding. If anything, this behavior was carried over from the brand of corrupt political practices that characterized English administration and politics in eighteenth and nineteenth century Ireland, with the reaping of emoluments and the bartering and selling of titles and position as commonplace as the sale of horses between two gentlemen. Because of a long history in dispensing with things connected to English law that simply made no sense, the Irish developed a survival tactic against abuses of English legal, social and political administrators by the effective use of the "personal relationship." To a country person in Ireland, a favor given was a favor reciprocated. It was not unusual to bestow upon a local magistrate or officer of the court presents of farm produce. This gave rise to the belief that by doing a man a favor, he would be glad to do one for you.[16] Once the initial shock of immigration and the process of developing the strong communal ties the Irish had known in their own country had been reestablished through the Church experience, the Irish would bring the custom of favor giving and doing to perfection in their religious and political practices. As principal religious leader of the Irish famine immigrant community, Hughes was looked upon as their natural hero, an immigrant who had arrived penniless as themselves, who had wielded a pickaxe before ever wielding a crozier, and who now more than ever, was the man to whom the favor of unquestioned fealty was bestowed by the masses of Irish Catholic immigrants. In return for this favor, Hughes, working on behalf of his people, became "more of a Roman gladiator than a devout follower of the meek founder of Christianity."[17] Ever the pragmatist, Hughes realized that in order to reset the broken bones of "the scattered debris of the Irish Nation,"[18] more than just churches and spiritual sustenance would be needed. Physical needs were acutely in need of being addressed in the form of food, medicine and employment. As time passed, it became evident that it was going to require greater resources to bring to bear on ameliorating the suffering of the immigrant population than the somewhat limited success that Hughes's European begging tours had garnered. He directed that his priests provide care for persons in public hospitals and poor houses. When the Jesuits arrived in New York, Hughes specifically directed that they focus their efforts on the charitable and penal institutions run by New York City on Wards Island. This directive immediately raised the hackles of nativist administrators, who interpreted the attempted incursion of priests into the social services system as an attack on the Protestant ministry. Hughes, hardened by the school fight, fought the civil authorities with the same argumentation he used against the New York Public School Society, that is, if Catholic priests are not permitted to engage in this kind of work, than clergymen of any religion should be barred as well. By this stage in Hughes's career, his opponents were fully aware that he was no longer a person who could be disregarded. In 1841, Hughes sponsored a group of laymen in the establishment of the Irish Immigration Society.

One of the initial aims of this organization was to raise money for the purpose of resettling the Irish on small plots of land out West. As this ultimately proved impractical, the Society endeavored to advise immigrants with respect to work, housing and the avoidance of persons who would swindle them out of their meager possessions. Because Hughes strongly believed that children were the prime targets of nativist Protestant proselytizing, he devoted intensive energy into the building of parochial schools. As critical as social institutions were to the survival of the Irish immigrant community, Hughes was still determined to show the world that even in the face of unspeakable anti-Catholic bigotry in America, the Church was still free. In doing so, he would build more than one hundred of them during the course of his reign as bishop and archbishop. In his frequent supplications to European missionary societies, Hughes would make the case that the justification of this program was that it gave not only to the Irish, but to every other bewildered immigrant: "It is only when he has the consolation of his religion within his reach that he feels comparatively happy in his new position. If on the Sunday he can be present at the Holy Sacrifice of the Mass. If only he can see the minister of his religion at the altar and hear the word of God in the language to which his ear was accustomed from childhood, he forgets that he is among strangers in a strange country."[19]

IV

A band of Philadelphia nativists, fresh from a rampage of marauding and the burning of St. Augustine's Church in Philadelphia, were to be welcomed with a public procession, courtesy of their sympathizers in New York. It was in this trying and most blatant excursion into the black hole of anti-Catholicism that Hughes struck a course of moderation, patience and sternness. Shortly after nativist activity in Boston prompted the burning of a convent in that city, the same act of villainy was prepared for St. Patrick's on Mott Street. Hughes wasted no time in vigorously planning to defend against the threatened attack. He started by having the sidewalks on all sides of the church building torn up and every window made ready for the hurling of projectiles. Next, members of the Ancient Order of Hibernians, a Catholic religious organization founded in Ireland in the 1500s for the purpose of protecting the Mass, the priest and the church, lined themselves up behind the churchyard walls armed with muskets. The would be nativist mob thought better of attacking the building, as they certainly knew that fatal bloodshed was the only possible outcome of such an act.

A meeting of the New York and Philadelphia native American groups was to be held in City Hall Park. Hughes made it clear through the *Freeman's Journal* that the scenes of Philadelphia were not going to be repeated in New York, and was known to have said to a priest who had been an eyewitness to the conflagration in Philadelphia that "if a single Catholic church was burned in New York City, the city would become a second Moscow."[20] Again, through the *Freeman's Journal,* Hughes sternly cautioned the Irish to stay away from the meeting. That the Irish were prepared to fight nativist Protestants was without question. There was no difference in the face of the foe, whether it be on Vinegar Hill in Wexford or the ramshackle, filthy streets of Sweeney's Shambles. While the Catholic churches of New York were sufficiently defended by a force of men willing to die, if necessary, in their defense, it was ultimately the steely and unintimidated determination of John Hughes that prevented the repeat of Philadelphia's unbridled violence in New York. In an extraordinary interview with New York Mayor, Robert Hunter Morris, Hughes, though not stated in tones of belligerency, nonetheless conveyed a sense of unmistakable consequences if city authorities failed to recognize the emergency and take appropriate action. That Bishop Hughes, head of a maligned and highly persecuted religion could psychologically reverse roles with the principal elected official of the city spoke volumes of the man who was unhesitating in taking on his foes. It was the words unsaid by Hughes that forced Mayor Morris to understand that nativist New Yorkers had much more to lose:

"Are you afraid," asked the mayor, "that some of your churches will be burned?"

"No," replied Hughes, "but I am afraid that some of yours will be burned. We can protect our own. I came to warn you for your own good."

"Do you think Bishop, that your people would attack the procession?"

"I do not, but the native Americans want to provoke a Catholic riot, and if they can do it in no other way, I believe they would not scruple to attack the procession themselves, for the sake of making it appear that the Catholics had assailed them."

"What then would you have me do?"

"I did not come here to tell you what to do. I am a churchman, not the Mayor of New York; but if I were the

Mayor, I would examine the laws of the state, and see if there were not attached to the police force a battery of artillery, a company of infantry and a squadron of horses; and I think I should find that if there were, and if so, I would call them out. Moreover, I should send to Mr. Harpur, the Mayor-elect, who has been chosen by the votes of this party. I should remind him that these men are his supporters; I should warn him that if they carry out their design, there will be a riot; and I urge him to use his influence in preventing his public reception of the delegates."[21]

As mayor, Morris clearly had an obligation to consider the safety of all New York's citizens. As a young man, he had attended the Washington Bible seminary and clearly was sympathetic to the anti-Catholic views of establishment nativism. There was no escaping however the determined Hughes. Morris was correct in perceiving Hughes to be the one man who held the keys to continued security and peace in New York. In this exchange with Morris, Hughes had achieved the high ground and never relinquished it. A less disciplined and less decisive person faced with the prospect of mayhem against his people and properties would have been cowed and intimidated. Knowing he was at a disadvantage with respect to dealing with the establishment did not prevent Hughes from asserting that he was prepared to go to the sword to defend his Church. In the end, there was no public demonstration and no confrontation. Hughes, through demonstrating an unparalleled courage and will, spared the city bloodshed, pillage, murder and the most unpleasant prospect of Christian using club and gun against Christian.

Shortly after the Morris interview, Bishop Hughes received a letter from a man who claimed to be the brother of George Shiffler, a Protestant who had been shot and killed during the outbreak of the recent violence in Philadelphia's Kensignton District. The author of the letter threatened Hughes with assassination, and although the signature on the letter was later determined to be that of a fictitious person, Hughes utilized its arrival as a means to excoriate the native American political and press arms. Hughes incorporated the contents of the letter into a public letter that he addressed to the mayor elect of New York, the Honorable James Harpur. Printed in the *Courier and Enquirer* on May 17th, 1844, Hughes denied the accusations made against him of being collusion with Whig political interests, of attempting to establish a separate Catholic political party and of trying to remove the Bible from the common schools. His invective spilled over to the *New York Herald* and the character of its editor, Mr. James Gordan Bennett. Hughes accused Bennett and his paper of fomenting the flames of unrest and asserted had there been a nativist riot in New York, Bennett and his publication would have been chiefly responsible. In another letter addressed by Hughes to Colonel William Stone, Hughes once again launched into ferocious invective about both Stone and Bennett, but principally about Bennett. Some Hughes supporters were horrified at the level of vitriol Hughes directed at both men, and implored him to write on more constructive matters such as the relationship of the Catholic Church with the civil government. Hughes, ever the ready combatant in the ongoing war against Roman Catholicism refused, and in a letter to his dear friend M.A. Frenaye, stated some of his reasons for not wanting to do so: "Bishop O'Connor has written to me, suggesting the propriety of an official exposition of Catholic principles; but there is one reason I mentioned to him against this, which is, that at this moment the malignity of the opposition will construe it an evidence of the species of understanding amongst ourselves and combination of ulterior purposes of which they already accuse us."[22]

Once again, the upsurge in nativist, anti-Irish and anti-Catholic sentiment and specifically, the actual outbreaks of violence against Catholics in places like Philadelphia and New York cast the vast differences between Hughes and his brother bishops into sharp relief. Perhaps this difference could once again be seen most sharply between Hughes and his brother Bishop in Philadelphia, Francis Kendrick. While Kendrick was the more influential in terms of the other bishops and the internal workings of the American Catholic Church, Hughes was certainly the one man to whom

Catholics looked to for leadership. Both men would continue to have impressive ecclesiastic careers, Kendrick becoming Archbishop of Baltimore and Hughes Archbishop of New York. Both men however approached their pastoral responsibilities from two totally different perspectives. Kendrick refused to authorize the arming of Catholics to defend themselves against nativist attacks, and on its face, would appear to have been a more recognizably Christian approach in dealing with the nativists than Hughes's threat to turn New York into a war zone if a single Catholic Church was harmed. The reality was that after days of violence in Philadelphia, Roman Catholic Church buildings had been torched to the ground, while not a single church in New York met the same fate. Another inescapable factor that accentuated the differences in style between the two prelates was that Philadelphians barely knew who the mild mannered and reserved Kendrick was. Except for the nativist burnings of churches in his diocese, Kendrick's name never appeared in newsprint. Anyone in New York who was capable of reading knew exactly who John Hughes was. As the events surrounding the nativist riots started to recede, Hughes returned to his role as pastor of souls. He continued dedicating new churches, and in one such instance where a church was being dedicated in Perth Amboy, New Jersey, Hughes apparently went to great lengths to explain the ceremony to the many Protestant curiosity seekers in attendance. He embarked upon a visitation of the western part of his sprawling diocese. He visited Buffalo and there the parishioners of St. Louis had been without a priest for two years. This situation was the result of the trustees having decided to exert control over the government of their parish in accordance with their believed right to control their own property. Bishop Hughes had other ideas. Just as in Philadelphia, the St. Louis parishioners went to the newspapers to amplify their grievance with Hughes and just as in Philadelphia, Hughes responded by removing the parish priest until such time as the parish leadership decided to conform to the dictates of the diocesan bishop. Having heard of the militant manner in which he had dealt with nativists, the trustees capitulated and tendered a public apology in the city newspapers. Never missing an opportunity for adding insult to injury, Hughes often made it a point to write the apologies out himself.[23]

As well as spiritual formation, Hughes was the creator and driving force behind the means of establishing material formation. As the Irish famine immigrant community began its slow assent to the latter of economic betterment, Hughes saw the need for his people to develop and learn the importance of thrift, savings and the ability to harness financial resources for the improvement of conditions related to those who remained in Ireland. The establishment of the Emigrant Savings Bank, created under the auspices of Hughes in conjunction with Irish bankers and merchants, most notably Eugene Kelly, was a milestone in the life of the post famine Irish immigrant community in New York City. Established at 51 Chambers Street, it opened its doors for business on September 30th, 1852. The first deposit of funds was made by Bridget White in the amount of one hundred dollars, a sum roughly equivalent to twenty-five hundred dollars in today's currency. Proud of her ability to make this deposit, the occasion for White may have passed without any further noteworthiness, except that when she was leaving the bank she encountered Hughes on his way into the bank to make a deposit himself.

The Emigrant bank was no ordinary financial institution. An outgrowth of the Irish Emigrant Society, which had been founded twelve years before in 1840 for the purpose of helping newly arrived Irish immigrants to find employment, housing and assistance with making remittances to family members in Ireland, the Emigrant Bank represented a first as it catered specifically to the needs of the Irish immigrant community. Whereas the previous medical, charitable, benevolent and church organizations represented the coordinated outreach to the Irish, The Emigrant bank represented a crucial step in the building of financial confidence and independence. As the principle depository not only for Irish immigrants but for parish funds and the personal savings accounts of many priests as well, the bank was soon thought of as "our" bank, a bank catering to the special needs of the Irish American community. By 1856, the bank could boast total deposits of $1,300,000.00. As always, Hughes and his clergy set a powerful example with respect to thrift and the importance of personal savings. The effect on his flock was immense, and also served as a means of providing relief for those who had been left behind in famine ravaged Ireland.[24]

In typical fashion, John Hughes had committed the fullness of his being to guiding, building and defending an immigrant church under attack. He had brought order from chaos, hope from hopelessness and steadiness from fear. He would be accused by his detractors both within and without the Catholic Church of utilizing high-handed tactics bordering on blatant demagoguery. His stance with respect to nativist aggression was bellicose and utterly un-Christian, but he never would have countenanced the turning of the other cheek. The results however of his chosen course of action were there for all to see: the political powers to be understood for the first time that properly organized and lead Roman Catholics represented more of a threat to the established order than merely a belief in transubstantiation. They also realized that Catholic churches and property, as far as New York anyway, were not going to be denigrated or put to the torch on Hughes's watch. They had finally met in John Hughes a man who had demonstrated the willingness to stand toe to toe with the most bigoted amongst them, and that he was a man preparing his people to take their place as Americans. In just a few more years, that preparedness would culminate on bloody Civil war battlefields with names like Antietam, Chancellorville and Gettysburg.

Chapter 7

America's Most Esteemed Catholic Churchman

As Hughes grew in stature and prominence as a Catholic Churchman, he developed relationships with many of America's most prominent political leaders. It was often said of him that had he lived in a different time, he may have achieved the stature of an ecclesiastic statesman such as Wolsey. Hughes was possessed of a penetrating intelligence and insight with respect to political matters, and he was often called upon to give counsel and provide advice on these matters to political figures of both major parties. One of the great distinguishing characteristics of Hughes was that he was never a man who courted the great and powerful; they always seemed to find their way to him.[1] One of the earliest examples of this tendency may be found in the person of Henry Clay, the Great Pacificator. Clay represented his state of Kentucky in both the House of Representatives and the United States Senate. He served three non-consecutive terms as speaker of the House as well as Secretary of State under John Quincy Adams from 1825 to 1829. He ran unsuccessfully for the Presidency in 1824, 1832 and 1844. During the presidential election of 1844, Clay's visit to New York City, prompted largely by the cordial letter received from former Governor William Seward, was encouraged by the apparent expressions of good will expressed by the bishop toward the Whig candidate: "The bishop was very kind and cordial... He desired me to assure you that he entertained the highest respect for you... that he was deeply impressed with the marked difference between your sentiments and political career and the sentiments and conduct of the intolerant Whigs who were made prominent by the party in New York City; and while he hoped for defeat on their Legislative ticket, he wished sincerely for the success of your Electoral ticket."[2] When Clay arrived in New York, Hughes and his secretary called on him at his hotel. The reception room was filled with dignitaries, politicians and prominent New Yorkers, but Clay unashamedly put them all out and sat in conversation with Hughes for over an hour. Clay parted Hughes's company that evening with great regret.[3]

Another prominent Whig politician of the era, and one who arguably represented the oldest and perhaps longest of intimate relationships enjoyed by Hughes with men of influence was William H. Seward. By extension, Hughes was to also befriend Seward's political handler from the time of his election as New York's governor, Thurlow Weed. The Seward-Weed-Hughes connection commenced at the time of the New York School Controversy, and over the course of twenty-three years wound its way to the Lincoln White House, and ultimately, to the heads of state of Catholic Europe.

William Henry Seward was a scion of wealth, born into and raised in a privileged childhood. Like Hughes, he was an energetic youth, who applied himself with a vitality and enthusiasm in school, in sports and in every social pursuit. His background however could not have been more different from the Roman Catholic prelate from Annaloghan, who was to become both confidant and intimate. Born on May 16th, 1801, just a little less than four years after Hughes, Seward's life was destined to be one of "preferment." While John Hughes lacked a Classical education, Seward would be subject to rigorous punishment for failure to properly translate passages from Caesar's War Commentaries or Virgil's poetry. Seward was immersed in a world of books in a way that Hughes could only have hoped for. Seward's social life, never impeded by the need to manage or work in gardens, was given to evenings visiting the neighbors where the sampling of apples, nuts and cider of his hometown of Florida, New York gave way to stimulating discussions about politics and religion. In later years, Seward would be noted for his entertainments, where guests were provided with the best of food, drink and conversation. The Seward family owned slaves, and in this they were not unlike other well-to-do families living in the area. Though his father permitted the family slaves to attend school with the Seward children, there were instances of the typical abuses heaped upon slaves in the form of whipping and forced wearing of an iron collar around the neck for acts of disobedience. In the same way that John Hughes detested having to oversee the slaves at Mount St. Mary's, Seward very early learned a marked repugnance for the institution of slavery as well.[4]

After completing his education and starting a law practice, the young Seward was drawn to the prospect of politics and public service. Finding the legal profession one of fairly dull and uninspired practice, fate would cross his path with a man who was to lead Seward not only through the portal of political life, but meticulously groom and guide him in his ascendancy from state senator, state governor and, ultimately, candidate for President of the United States. Thurlow Weed was more like Hughes in background and makeup than his sophisticated and highly educated pupil Seward.

Raised in poverty, Weed's family was forced to move from one location to another, that is, when his father was not in prison for debt. Deprived of all but a few years of formal schooling, the young Weed was forced at an early age to work in order to help ameliorate the family's dire financial condition. Like Hughes, he fought to educate himself with an intensity that bordered on the fanatical. He ravished books, sometimes walking miles to borrow them. Like Hughes, he constantly sought to assess his strengths and weaknesses, working with intensity to eliminate the weaknesses. Where Hughes focused on the strengthening of his oratorical and writing abilities, Weed sought to train and discipline his memory. Drawn to politics, Weed found the ideals of the growing American Republic in developing its resources, improving roads and infrastructure, imposing protective tariffs and extending its dominions. It was in the person of Henry Clay that these ideas would meld into the "American

System" and the Whig Party. Both men would be greatly successful in their personal enrichment endeavors, for Hughes would gain national notoriety by virtue of debating, and Weed was to achieve phenomenal recall. Both men also possessed a strong native intelligence, energy, warmth of personality and the ability to fearlessly carve out their respective powerful niches. Weed would go on to achieve success as a printer, publisher and, ultimately, as a powerful political boss. Weed would be known as the "Dictator," an appellation some would assert aptly fit Hughes as well.

It was the School Controversy "that brought Governor Seward and myself to acquaintance with the bishop, and was the basis of a friendship both alike endearing and enduring."[5]

At the time of the New York Assembly election during the School Controversy, supporters of Hughes's position on the right of Catholics to receive a portion of the tax monies for Catholic school education realized that opposition to the measure was in both the Whig As well as Democratic parties. Hughes called for the support of the special slate to be known as the Carrol Hall candidates, and Weed recorded the mighty determination in which Hughes pursued that objective: "I dined with the bishop that day, but I did not think it expedient to accompany him to the Hall. I went however unobserved into the gallery, where I listened with intense interest to his bold and telling speech to a crowded and enthusiastic auditory. After explaining clearly and forcibly the truly enlightened and philanthropic recommendations of Governor Seward, and dwelling eloquently upon the blessings which it was designed to extend to poor, neglected orphan children, he told his hearers that most of the candidates in nomination by both Whig and Democratic convention were opposed to school reform."[6]

Seward, himself the subject of intense revilement and opposition due to his beliefs concerning the school question, wrote Hughes a few days after the Carroll Hall candidates garnered a total of twenty-two hundred votes in the Assembly elections of 1841. Though an insufficient amount to win, it was enough to show that Catholics were ready to act in a united fashion to obtain recourse through the

political system for the righting of injustice and the legitimate advancement of Catholic issues: "I thank you very
sincerely for your kind letter of the 8th, and am exceedingly
gratified in learning that you bear with true philosophy the
buffeting of the short-sighted leaders of faction. I have no
concern for your ultimate vindication. It is your fortune as
well as mine that philanthropic conceptions for the improvement of society come in conflict with existing interests
founded in existing prejudices... The session of the legislature approaches. I will say to you with all freedom, that I
propose to reassert my opinions and principles with firmness, and to submit the subject of educational system to the
direct action of the Legislature. May I hope that your
concern on that great subject will induce you to accede to
my wishes by making me a brief visit... Do not say nay."[7]
Governor Seward, true to his word, did not forget the
promise he made to address the school agenda in the new
legislative session. Writing to Hughes not long after the
session opened, Seward enthusiastically reported that "The
most gratifying indications present themselves on every
side."[8]

The opposition never desisted in attempting to establish
a conspiratorial link between Hughes and Seward, accusing
the former of bartering Catholic votes in exchange for
Seward and Weed doing the exclusive bidding of Catholics.
In like fashion, the Locofoco faction of the Democratic Party
became alarmed especially as it became apparent that they
would no longer enjoy the Catholic vote, especially the Irish
component, unless they acted in ways to earn it. In forging
this early relationship with William Seward and Weed,
Hughes would stand convicted of the false charges of trying
to launch a Catholic political party, blur the lines of church
and state to suit Catholic ends through the help of complicit
politicians and worse, lead the way to Popish domination of
the American way of life.

I

Aside from winning recognition on the religious front for his outspoken and unrepentant defense of American Catholicism, Hughes was simultaneously emerging as a quintessential voice of American national interest. He preached a gospel of the "isms:"Catholicism, Americanism and patriotism. He ardently supported the war against Mexico in 1846-48. Hughes supported the administration of President James K. Polk, even in a war pitting Catholic immigrants against their Mexican coreligionists. Yet within the United States army of the period, there were no Catholic chaplains charged with ministering to the souls of the Faithful. The presence of priests was forbidden and Catholic soldiers were forced to attend Protestant services. In addition, Catholic troops were forced to suffer the indignities born of the common prejudices held by most of the U.S. army's officer corps.

The Mexican government was well aware of the strong anti-Catholic bias that existed north of the border, and actively offered to give American Catholic immigrants willing to desert and take up arms against the American enemy grants of land as a reward.

Upwards of 25 percent of General Zachary Taylor's expeditionary force was made up of Irish Catholics. Polk keenly recognized the tremendous power and influence of Hughes, and through his Secretary of State, James Buchanan, the stage was set for Hughes to be engaged in national affairs beyond what any Catholic Church leader had ever been asked to do.

The Sixth Provincial Council of the American Bishops convened at Baltimore in May of 1846. At that time, Bishop Hughes received a letter from Buchanan, inviting him to Washington, D.C. at the request of the President to consult with the government "on affairs of importance." News of the actual outbreak of hostilities with Mexico had reached Washington on the very day the Council opened. Rumors had been circulating that Hughes was to be tapped as a special envoy to Mexico, and while nothing specifically of the sort was contained in Buchanan's correspondence, Hughes decided to broach the possibility of such a mission with his brother bishops. Ostensibly, they all concurred that if that was the intent of the invitation, Hughes should in no way consider accepting unless it carried the full rank and title of a diplomatic representative. Buchanan knew Hughes well. He had often made reference to their common Irish heritage, both men being connected to the province of Ulster. "It occurred to the President, to whom I am indebted for the particulars of this affair, whilst the bishop was in Washington, and most probably at an earlier period, that, should he consent to visit Mexico, he might render essential services in removing the violent prejudices of the Mexicans, and especially of their influential clergy, which then prevailed against the United States, and thus prepare the way for peace between the two republics. In this I heartily concurred. Independently of his exalted character as a dignitary of the Church, I believed him to be one of ablest and most accomplished and energetic men I have ever known, and that he possessed all the prudence and firmness necessary to render such a mission successful."[9] On meeting Hughes, Polk recorded in his diary: "Bishop Hughes called with Mr. Buchanan at seven o'clock. Mr. Buchanan, having already conversed with me on the subject, retired and I held a conversation for an hour with him. I fully explained to him the objections which we would probably encounter from the prejudices of the Catholic priests in Mexico and that our object was to not to overthrow their religion and rob their churches. Bishop Hughes fully agreed with me in the opinion that it was important to remove such impressions. I said that it was the great object of my desiring to have this interview with him to ask whether some of the priests of the United States who spoke the Spanish language could be induced to accompany our army as chaplains. Bishop Hughes at once said that having a few catholic priests with the army would have a good effect, and expressed his entire willingness to cooperate with the government in giving such aid as was within his power. I found Bishop Hughes a highly intelligent and agreeable man, and my interview with him was of the most satisfactory character."[10]

When news of the proposed mission became public, Protestant circles erupted in unbridled furor over the prospect of an American President sending a Roman Catholic bishop on a diplomatic mission. A scathing editorial by the bitterly anti-Catholic *Church Times* publication summed up in irate terms the proposed appointment: "A Presbyterian President calls upon a Roman Catholic bishop to give assistance in a state affair. Mr. Polk has involved his country in a war, and notwithstanding the great horror which men of his stamp feel of the encroachments of Rome, he does not scruple to give her a pretense for interference even at the center of government, by soliciting her good offices to protest the American army from anticipated foes... We shall see the end when the end comes. But meanwhile, it may be interesting for observers of the times to watch the course of the incipient court paid by the state to the Church of Rome."[11]

In like fashion, editorials started appearing in other anti-Catholic publications, alarmed at such developments. In *The Herald*, loath to believe that Hughes or anyone like him could be selected and sent on such a mission, attempted to create an atmosphere of conspiratorial intrigue between Polk and Hughes: "We have received intelligence from an authentic source in Washington that negotiations of a perfectly astounding character are in progress between the Right Rev. John Hughes, Bishop of New York, and the President of the United States. We have the particulars before us and will probably publish them in a few days when we get a fuller and more detailed account. This affair, when published, will be far more interesting and create greater excitement among all classes, and more especially among the anti-Catholic portion of the community, than even the Awful Disclosures of Maria Monk or any other awful disclosures that have been published in the last fifty years. This new and extraordinary move of Bishop Hughes will cause a good deal of astonishment."[12]

Hughes was circumspect over the incident, never fully disclosing the interview with Polk in other than very general terms. The reality was that Hughes felt it would have been totally inappropriate to reveal anything he had discussed with the President of the United States. He was no doubt flattered and gratified that such consideration would have been accorded him, however; Hughes had neither the ambition nor the desire to go to Mexico. In his heart he believed he was duty bound to serve his country, but at the same time, "as a Christian bishop, I am bound to be a servant of the peace; but I have no favors to ask from any, and I have important objects to fill at home."[13]

II

Hughes's singular gifts of mind and mission, together with uncompromising love of his Catholic Faith and adopted nation insured his prominence in all the important religious and social developments of his time. Purcell of Cincinnati may have been admired for his tact and unassuming spirit of benevolence; Kendrick, for his scholarship and diplomacy. Only Hughes was perceived as the lightening rod. He had emerged as the Catholic Bishop to fear because his opponents knew that he would answer their threats of force with force, physically as well as intellectually. No ecclesiastic figure of his day possessed a more statesmanlike appreciation and knowledge of the American commonwealth; no man of his day displayed a greater confidence in the belief that America was truly the one true haven for men who yearned to breathe free. He looked at the United States as the refuge for those who sought to throw of the manacles of poverty and political oppression. Even in the darkest hours of nativist scorn and attack, the unbridled confidence and belief in America never faltered. In addition to his episcopal duties, Hughes, without thought of accolade or recompense, continued to direct his extraordinary oratorical abilities, his talents as a conversationalist and his ability to command the written word as the means of battling injustice and oppression.

In 1847, at the invitation of John C. Calhoun and Stephen A. Douglas, Hughes was invited to Washington D.C. to preach to Congress. The invitation addressed to the prelate stated as follows:

"Sir, the undersigned members of Congress respect-
fully invite you to preach in the Hall of the House of
Representatives on Sunday next (12th inst.) at 11
o'clock, unless some other hour of the day may be
more agreeable to you... We are, Right Rev. Sir, your
obedient servants."[14]

The invitation included the names of some twenty members of the U.S. Senate and thirty-three members of the
House of Representatives. On December 9th, Speaker of the
House, Robert C. Winthrop added the following addendum
to the previously issued invite:

"It gives me great pleasure to place the Hall of the
House of Representatives at the service of Bishop
Hughes, in conformity with the above inviatation."[15]

In his acceptance, Hughes replied "I do not feel at liberty
to decline a compliance with a wish so kindly expressed on
your part and so flattering to me. I have the honor, to
remain, gentlemen, your Obedient servant, John Hughes,
Bishop of New York."[16] Constant themes stressed by Hughes
were Americanism and the virtue of good citizenship. A
charge constantly hurled at Hughes by enemies was that he
led people who were incapable of understanding or practicing the principles of a democratic republic... that their
allegiances belonged to a foreign potentate in Rome. It was
fitting therefore that on the day of Hughes's epochal sermon
on December 12th, he chose as a topic "Christianity":
"Beloved brethren, it was at quite a late period of the week
that I was honored with the invitation, which I prize so
highly, to address you from this place. I had already
consented to speak in one of our churches, where my
presence would have been more natural and more expected;
and for the place I had prepared, by reflection, some
remarks on a subject which I would not deem suitable, on
the present occasion; for I should feel that I corresponded
but poorly to a compliment so much to be valued, if I could
obtrude upon you any reflections or arguments upon these
doctrinal subjects, which to great an extent, have divided

the Christian world. Allow me then to make some reflections upon *Christianity and its Author, as containing and setting forth the germ of moral, social and political regeneration in this fallen world of ours.*[17] Hughes's address was an unmistakable call to his fellow Christians assembled in the House Chamber to acknowledge the one Divine Truth and one Divine mission of every Christian, regardless of denomination: "It is only in the divine morality of the Christian faith that we are furnished with a worthy motive to a virtuous and holy life. There we are taught that God is our reward – that he is the rewarder of those who seek him – that he will punish your injustice toward your brethren – that He has so honored His disciples as to place Himself, as it were, in their stead, declaring as the beneficent Redeemer of man has declared, "Whatsoever you do unto these little ones, ye do even unto Me."[18]

In furtherance of the positive, pervasive and all influencing attributes of the Christian faith, Hughes asked if not all of the noblest endeavors of men and governments are not tied back to the notion of the all present and powerful Christian God: "Do you speak of the rights of nations, of the sanctity of the first government, the family, and the holiness of the domestic law. Have they not all felt the hallowed influence of the religion of peace and love? Where among the ancients do you find public provision for the poor? Where were the hospitals of heathen civilization? Where do you behold houses in which to gather the broken and trampled reeds of human misfortune? Where do you find war regulated by a spirit of humanity? Where do you find recognition of the rights of nations, or of individual man? Nowhere. And in vain do you search for any other origin of those blessings than that source from whence they sprang: God established the word of his eternal justice, through the medium of his Divine Son, upon the earth, holding man to a just accountability for his crimes, and making virtue so sweet that the very sacrifices which it demands become themselves the recompense of its exercise."[19] Perhaps reflecting upon his own feelings with respect to his adopted land, Hughes appropriately proclaimed that, "If a man would serve his country, his fellow man, if he would procure to himself the highest enjoyment of which his own nature is capable, he will be more studious of the comforts, rights and interests of others than his own."[20] This sentiment no doubt was also reflective of a deeper hope of Hughes, namely, that his Church and the people of that Church would one day be accepted fully as members of a country destined to be a beacon light of the world. In closing, Hughes gave life to this hope in a touching prayer: "...and now I would breathe a prayer to God, that he will preserve you [Congress], and that you, above all, to whom the nation and the world look with so much confidence, may be guided in your deliberations by the Spirit of God; that you may be enlightened where light is necessary, and swayed in your judgement in favor of those decisions which will at once promote the glory of our common Father, and the interest of this great and growing country, whose destinies may exercise hereafter so important an influence upon the nations of the earth."[21]

While Hughes was growing in stature beyond his Diocesan See, his flock was also growing. By virtue of the Irish fleeing the famine, the Catholic Church in New York was to experience exponential growth between 1846 and 1851, as an estimated one million souls made the Atlantic crossing from Ireland.

In 1849, the only American Sees that enjoyed metropolitan dignity were Baltimore, Oregon City and St. Louis. In May, one of the major items addressed by the Seventh Council of Baltimore was the need for creation of three more archbishoprics, namely in New Orleans, Cincinnati and New York. Though pressing given the growing American Church, the Pontiff had been forced to delay consideration on action facilitating this request because of the political problems in Italy. On October 3rd, 1850, a papal brief was received by Bishop Hughes at the Mulberry Street residence advising that New York had been raised to the dignity of an archbishopric, and Hughes to the dignity of its first archbishop. As part of this development, the bishops of Boston, Hartford, Albany and Buffalo would be his suffragans. He made the announcement at St. Patrick's during mass the following Sunday, and advised the assembled congregation that he would be departing for Rome to personally receive the pallium[22] from the Pope. As a further sign of respect and recognition of Hughes as the most prominent American Catholic prelate, his farewell visits with friends in both Philadelphia and Washington resulted in an invitation to dine with President Millard Fillmore and his family. On the eve of his departure to Rome he wrote a pastoral letter that alluded to the great honor that had been bestowed upon himself and New York but, more specifically, about the deep importance of Catholic education for both the laity as well as those contemplating a vocation to the priesthood: "The education of Catholic youth in a Catholic manner, to which we have so often called to your attention, should still be the object of your anxious care. Wherever it is possible, whether in city or town, or rural district, let the Catholic priest and Catholic parents organize Catholic schools for the training of youth. We would also exhort the reverend clergy to superintend, from time to time, by personal inspection, the progress and working of these schools, and not leave them altogether to the direction of the teacher, however worthy of confidence he may be.... More recently, and even up to the present time, our ecclesiastical students, the recruits of the sanctuary, have come, in a great measure, from the same sources, but we cannot look to the zeal of other countries for the perpetuation of our clergy.... We therefore exhort Christian parents to cherish in their children signs of vocation to the priesthood, and we exhort you, beloved brethren of the clergy, to encourage this spirit in the families of your respective congregations."[23]

The decade of the 1850s in America dawned with the sectional differences between North and South growing wider. The issue of slavery was intensifying and differences with respect to acknowledgement of southern rights concerning the "peculiar institution" was meeting more and more with an inflexible response from abolitionist sentiment in the North. Hughes was an avid anti-abolitionist. He detested abolitionism as an extreme position because in his view, he believed that the immediate freeing of slaves into American society would ultimately do them irreparable harm. Hughes further detested abolitionism because of its blatant hypocrisy; many that espoused freedom for slaves on moral grounds were simultaneously anti-immigrant. Additionally, masses of freed slaves would represent serious economic competition for those at the bottom of the economic ladder, which translated into large numbers of Irish Catholics presided over spiritually by Hughes. Allegations by militant abolitionists that Hughes was pro-secession and anti-Union breathed life into the notion that groups like the Irish were nothing more than surrogates of the Pope, incapable of absorbing and living in accordance with American democratic principles. Nothing could have been further from the truth. Perhaps the real reason for renewed vitriol against Hughes and the Catholic Church lay not so much with Hughes's position on slavery as much as the realization that in the south, Hughes's anti-abolitionist position not only won him respect but mitigated attacks against his Church and Catholics. On the other hand, members of the Catholic clergy, consistent with centuries of teaching and tradition, were themselves slaveholders. While the Catholic clergy believed that slaves be fed proper food, given education and provided the benefit of family association, they never agitated for an end of the institution. Hughes saw the issue as a direct challenge to the Constitutional guarantee of a man's right to his property, especially in places where the institution had already existed. To Hughes, slavery was an issue of States Rights, the domain where the issue both properly belonged and should remain. Knowing his own background with respect to the status of Catholics in Ireland, it is inconceivable that Hughes could have ever been a personal supporter of slavery, as he knew well from experience the degradation and humiliation that accompanies servitude. He was primarily a practical leader politically as well as spiritually. His anti-abolitionist views brought reprieve for his people in certain quarters, a novelty not to be overlooked given the anti-Catholic climate of the times.

III

After assumption of his appointment, Hughes embarked on a trans-Atlantic voyage to Rome for his official investiture as Archbishop of New York by Pope Pius IX. After a short stay in England, where he was accorded great honors, he arrived in the Eternal City on Christmas Eve, 1850. The newly minted archbishop had not been long in Rome when rumors began surfacing of his being made a cardinal. The matter was certainly under discussion within the inner precincts of the Vatican power structure. The suggestion of Hughes's elevation to cardinal however was more the product of American, rather than Roman suggestion. The U.S. government was not unaware of the desire of Pope Pius IX to make the College of Cardinals more universal. For reasons that were more political than spiritual, certain members of President Fillmore's cabinet saw an extremely beneficial aspect of so designating a member of the American Catholic clergy to receive such an honor by the Church. It was generally understood that should such an event take place, Hughes was to be considered the most desirable of all possible candidates. The Vatican machinery however was far more circumspect on the matter than the United States would give credit for. Rome, given the anti-Catholic history of the American Republic, was not about to cede to American politicians say so in who would or would not become a prince of the Church.

While Hughes was treated in Rome with the utmost of care and respect, even by the Pope, conferring of the cardinal's red hat was still a prize beyond an American's reach. The accolade was not to be bestowed upon Hughes. The ceremony of conferring the pallium however was carried out on April 3rd, 1851. With all of the pomp and circumstance of the Church of Rome, Pius himself performed the ceremony. For Hughes, it could not have been interpreted as anything other than an act of the greatest kindness and recognition for so esteemed a churchman. Prior to his departure to New York on June 11th, Hughes was feted by the Catholic community of Liverpool, England. Never before had an episcopal leader of the Roman Catholic Church received such acclaim. Archbishop Hughes, deeply touched and gratified to be the object of such heartfelt adulation, was nonetheless grateful to be embarking on his return voyage to New York City. He arrived home on June 22nd and spent several days visiting schools, colleges and religious institutions. On July 1st, he preached a sermon at St. Patrick's outlining the high points of his visitation to Rome. On July 21st, prominent members of the New York Catholic community gave Hughes a grand banquet in the Astor House. It was a fitting end to his promotion to archbishop, as well as a genuine outpouring of the affection and esteem he was held in my members of his diocese. That Hughes commanded so prominent a position in the broader community was unquestionable as the following incident demonstrates.[24]

In the spring of 1853, Rome dispatched Monsignor Gaetano Bedini, Archbishop of Thebes, as Apostolic Nuncio to the court of the Brazils, charging him with stopping to visit the President of the United States to deliver a complimentary autograph letter from Pope Pius IX. He was also charged with the task of ascertaining the state of the Catholic Church in the United States with respect to its prospects and needs. On March 19th, preparatory to Bedini's arrival, Cardinal Antonelli, Secretary of State for the Holy See had written to the American charge in Rome, Lewis Cass, Jr., with respect to the impending visit:

"The undersigned, Cardinal Secretary of State, has the honor to inform the Charges D'Affaires of the United States, Monsignor Bedini, Archbishop of Thebes and Apostolic Nuncio near the Imperial Court of the Brazils, has been instructed to proceed to the United States and to compliment at this juncture in the name of the Holy Father, the President of the United States."[25]

A few days later, Lewis Cass, Jr., wrote to Cardinal Antonelli that Bedini would receive a most gracious welcome in the United States:

"The undersigned, Charges D'Affaires of the United States of America has the honor to acknowledge the reception of the communication, dated March 19th of His Eminence, the Cardinal Secretary of State, which announces the coming departure of Monsignor Bedini, Archbishop of Thebes and Apostolic Nuncio to the Imperial Court of the Brazil, who is charged with a complimentary mission to the President of the United States of America. The undersigned has received this intelligence with the most lively interest and hastened to communicate it to his government. Assuring in advance, your Eminence, of the cordial reception Monsignor Bedini will receive from his government, and of the extreme pleasure, which the President of the United States will receive from the favorable expression of the sentiments of the Holy Father, the undersigned takes this occasion to express to you his highest consideration."[26]

Bedini arrived in New York on the 30th of June, and after spending several days with Archbishop Hughes at the Mulberry Street residence, proceeded in the company of Hughes to Washington where he had a most gratifying interview with President Franklin Pierce. After Washington, Hughes and Bedini travelled west to Milwaukee, where Bedini preached at the consecration of that city's newly erected cathedral. The two also travelled to Green Bay, Montreal and finally to Saratoga. By this time it was late August, and Hughes returned to New York, having been gone for well over a month. Bedini joined Hughes in October, where he remained until the onset of winter. During this period, Bedini availed himself of the many great gestures of hospitality shown him by the Catholic community as well as fully participating in any major ceremonies and events of a significant religious nature.

Hughes had been greatly encouraged by the excellent reception Bedini had received, as he was a prelate most interested in seeing a fuller and more harmonious relationship evolve between the government of the United States and the Holy See. Such sentiment was clearly reflected in a reply sent by the Vatican to Hughes on the recent success of the Bedini visit: "With regard to Monsignor Bedini, I considered to have your letter all translated by an Italian. I gave a copy of it to the *sostituto di stato*, Monsignor Berardi, who is a particular friend of mine; he read it to the Pope, who was delighted beyond measure at the news about Monsignor Bedini.... His Eminence feels very much obliged to your grace for the active and prudent part you have taken in promoting both the dignity of the Holy See and the good of religion."[27] At this juncture however, the Bedini mission took a disastrous turn for the worst.

Throughout the spring of 1853, nativist groups had been gathering steam under names such as "*The Friends of Civil and Religious Liberty*" and "*The American and Foreign Christian Union.*" The basis of this new wave of unrest had been spurred by the invitation of another foreigner to American shores, and ex-priest from Bologna, Italy by the name of Alessandro Gavazzi. A veteran of the revolution of 1848, this embittered man moved to England, converted to Protestantism and devoted the full measure of his existence to the condemnation of the Catholic Church and the Papacy. He was cast as the male version of "Maria Monk,"[28] and his arrival on the scene coincided with what was to be a request for the United States to consider receiving a papal nuncio, or formal representative of the Holy See to the United States.

In the wake of the glowing reviews on Bedini, Hughes had written to James Campbell, Postmaster General of the United States, himself a Catholic, about the possibility of establishing a papal nunciature representing the Holy See. The United States had established relations with Rome during the Polk administration, with the appointment of a minister to the Papal States, that is, the non-religious aspect of the Pope's domain. Campbell's reply to Hughes was both disappointing but hardly unexpected: "In relation to the establishment of a nunciature in this country, the president will receive a charge or minister from the Pope, but he can only of course be received as his political representative. If his holiness were to appoint a layman, there would be no difficulty in receiving him in the same manner as the representative of every other sovereign now received – charge of course only with the public affairs of the Pontifical States."

Clearly, it was evident that the Vatican's perceptions of the state of Catholicism and the reality of religious and civil matters in the American Republic were being viewed through very different lenses. Had the United States been a Catholic country such as France or Spain, appointment of a papal "nuncio" would have been *de riguer*. The United States however was not a Catholic country, a reality not readily grasped by the Roman pontiff for a variety of reasons.

For one, the perception of the Vatican with respect to the growth of the Catholic Church was flawed. Growth was perceived as the result of conversions of Protestants to Catholicism, something which was clearly not the case. The reality was that growth of the American Catholic Church had primarily been the result of the influx of huge numbers of immigrants, mostly from Ireland, with a significant number having come from Germany as well. Another misconception of the Vatican stemmed from the organization of the Catholic Church itself in America. The American hierarchy was by definition relatively young in comparison to its European counterparts. Sees were being established so quickly that oftentimes very young and hardly experienced priests were being promoted to the ranks of the episcopacy in order to keep up with the ever widening expansion. Councils were frequently being called, and the numerous referrals of incidents and complaints being forwarded for adjudication and review led to the conclusion on Rome's part that there was need for closer scrutiny of the American Church and its green hierarchy. Of greatest concern to Rome were issues that touched on the trustee situation, which not only had given rise in the past to organizational chaos and breech of discipline, but stoked the ever pervasive fear and repercussion of public scandal, as in Philadelphia. Having a nuncio appointed would, in the eyes of the Pope, have gone a long way in blunting the negative effects of such problems and at the same time providing the means for tighter control of American Catholic affairs. In a Protestant country however, the papal nuncio would have had nothing to do.[29] That a clerical representative of the Catholic Church would even be suggested for accreditation in Washington was enough kerosene in the early 1850s to spark the flames of anti-Catholicism anew. Before Hughes had actually received the reply from Postmaster General Campbell, Bedini took it upon himself to undertake visiting various parts of the United States again. This time however he was unaccompanied. For health reasons, Hughes had decided to embark upon a restorative visit to the Island of Cuba.

It was no secret that many members of the American hierarchy did not look favorably upon the Bedini visit and their worst fears were about to be once again vindicated. At each of Bedini's stops in Cincinnati, Baltimore, Boston and New York, he was being hounded by the radical ex-cleric Gavazzi. Following Bedini, he fomented hysteria by his claims that Bedini was the "Butcher of Bologona," responsible for the imprisonment and execution of hundreds of freedom loving Italian nationalists. A self-styled imitator of Allesandro Gavazzi, named John C. Orr, led a campaign of violence against the Catholic Church throughout the New England region that included church burnings and assault on members of the Catholic clergy. In one instance, a priest in a remote village in Maine was tarred and feathered. In Louisville Kentucky, anti-Catholic mobs descended on churches and put them to the torch under the false pretext that one church was storing arms in its basement in anticipation of a Catholic uprising to take place at the signal of the Pope's representative in Washington. Clearly, the Bedini mission had outworn its welcome, and his travels incited a level of violence against Catholics not seen in a decade.

Bedini returned to New York and he set about arranging to travel not to the country which he was to be nuncio, Brazil, but rather, back to Rome. Again, newspapers publishers such as Horace Greeley continued to fan the flames of anti-Catholic sentiment by headlining a story to the effect that a young girl had been forced into a convent of the Sisters of Mercy in Providence, Rhode Island. As news of Bedini's return to New York spread, Catholics once again prepared to fend off attacks from marauding groups of nativists. Anti-Pope meetings materialized everywhere, and a

large group of Irish assembled at the residence of Archbishop Hughes until the early hours of morning in anticipation of having to defend it from attack. Both the *Herald*
and *Tribune* printed a statement signed by seventy-seven
Italian nationalists accusing Bedini of the proscriptions,
signed in his hand, against liberty loving revolutionaries in
Bologna. On January 28th, Metropolitan Hall was burnt to
the ground. Because Gavazzi had lectured there, the rumor
was quickly spread that the fire was an act of retaliation by
Catholics. In Boston, rumor had spread that the besieged
Italian Archbishop had slipped into the city undetected with
the idea of secretly sailing from that port. In the evening, an
anti-Catholic crowd numbering close to 500 persons burned
Bedini in effigy. Many waited at the docks hoping to be able
to burn the man for real. In truth, Bedini was still in New
York and for fear that another major riot would erupt due to
his presence, he was secretly smuggled across to Staten
Island with the aid of Father Jeremiah Cummings. It was
then he composed a bitter letter to Hughes about the most
unwelcome reception her had been accorded.

Bedini, hardly masking his feelings concerning the treatment he had been accorded by both American press and
public, sarcastically alluded to Hughes's popularity among
the Cubans. Having studied and developed fluency in Spanish, Hughes had toured churches, preached and mingled
amongst the Cuban people to great effect, causing Bedini to
reflect how "he trusted he would find every comfort in a land
ruled by a monarchy, whereas, it seemed a democracy was
unable to lawfully protect strangers."[30] Still, in spite of the
bitterness expressed by Bedini, he still retained his affection
for and gratitude for Hughes, expressing in his reports back
to Rome his conviction that Hughes should be considered for
the College of Cardinals: "Everyone knows that the Archbishop of New York, Monsignor Hughes, is a skillful orator,
and this quality, together with his resolute spirit and untir-
ing energy, has put him on the top not only in estimation of
Catholics but of the whole nation. He enjoys in America the
highest regard and influence, and this is due to the pulpit
and the press."[31] It is ironic that Francis Kendrick, the
Roman trained doyen of the American Catholic Church,

Archbishop of America's primal See of Baltimore, theologian, scholar and conciliator was not the first recipient of the embattled Italian's adulation... not even the second: "After him," concluded Bedini, "ranks the bishop of Pittsburg."[32]

Hughes was furious over the manner in which Bedini was forced to leave the country, and summoning the defender's mentality so effectively demonstrated by him over the course of the last two decades wrote Bedini telling him that "If I had been in New York we should have taken a carriage at my door, even an open one if the day had been fine enough, and gone by the ordinary streets to the steamboat on which you were to embark."[33] Safely back in the Eternal City and no doubt greatly relieved in the knowledge that the Archbishop of New York had been sidelined in Cuba during the worst of the protestations against himself, Bedini must have breathed a tremendous sigh of relief in the knowledge that riding the streets of New York in an open carriage on a fine day with John Hughes was an experience he was able to forgo.[34]

Chapter 8

Preserving the Union

The origins of the American Civil War were complex issues stemming from different understandings of Federalism, States' Rights, cultural perspectives, and ultimately, the growing power of the slaveholding interest. In 1787, the delegates to the Constitutional Convention were reluctant to deal with the slavery question in a permanent fashion because of its divisive nature, and fearing failure to win ratification by the southern states, stipulated that the matter was to be held in abeyance until the year 1808. This was the first of a series of events to prevent definitively dealing with the slavery issue. The hope was that eventually the need for slaves would lessen, slaves would be voluntarily emancipated by their masters, and slaves themselves would eventually opt to return voluntarily to Africa from where they originally came. This was not to be the case, as the Southern economy, vastly different from the North's emerging industrial development and wage based labor system became more and more dependent upon human beings to harvest cash crops like cotton. African slaves were ideally suited to the hot and humid climate of the South and ending slavery would have resulted in economic chaos. Trafficking in slavery was eventually outlawed in many states by 1804, but there were never any provisions made with respect to the slaves already held. The framers of the Constitution saw an inevitable clash between the power of the Federal (national) government and the rights of individual states. Content to only ban the further importation of slaves, there was no will for tampering with the institution of slavery in the places where it already existed. From this unresolved dilemma would emerge bitterly strident sectional differences between North and South in the decades to follow. Between 1847 and 1854, newly created territories organized and applied for statehood. The burning question would ultimately come down to whether they would be admitted to the Union as "free" or "slave." The most contentious legislation pointing to this bitter divide emerged at the time of introduction of the Kansas-Nebraska Act. Neither the Missouri Compromise of 1820 nor the more complex and equally indecisive Compromise of 1850 held out the prospect of a permanent solution to the problem of slavery. Both were merely stopgap measures in the deadly and growing bitterness and resentment between the country's two halves. By the middle of the 1850s, many members of both houses of the Congress were attending sessions of their respective bodies armed with pistols and other weapons.[1] The Northern and Southern states were on the brink of civil war.

By 1860, the country was irrevocably divided with respect to the slavery question, the expansion of slavery and the rights of slaveholders. It was during this momentous presidential election year that events would come to a head. The presidency was contested in a four party race consisting of the Northern Democrats, whose presidential candidate was Illinois Senator Stephen A. Douglas; John C. Breckenridge, candidate of the Southern Democrats; John Bell of the Constitutional Union Party and the Republican Party candidate, Abraham Lincoln. The Republican Party had unsuccessfully fielded its first presidential candidate in the election of 1856, John C. Fremont.

Much however had changed in both the tone and mood of the country in the four years between elections, and the Republicans were now front and center with respect to national leadership on the burning question of slavery. Republican domination in many northern states guaranteed Lincoln, an outsider, with a sufficient number of electoral votes to win. This would happen in spite of the fact that throughout most of the Southern states, Lincoln's name didn't even appear on the ballot. In November of 1860,

Abraham Lincoln was elected the 16th President of the United States. Of the thirty-one states that comprised the United States at that time, Lincoln carried a total of eighteen, garnishing one hundred eighty electoral votes and a popular vote of 1,865,908. By the time of his inauguration on March 4th, 1861, a total of seven southern states, with South Carolina in the lead, had seceded from the Union.[2] The time of compromise had passed. From the very beginning of the Republic, the seeds of dissension over slavery had been planted. The dreaded contest had been successfully placated or held in abeyance in each generation since the founding of the nation. Sadly, the compromises and great statesman who fashioned those compromises were dead. It now seemed as if the age of rational men had died as well.

I

Abraham Lincoln was an enigma in American politics. He served but a single term in the House of Representatives (1847-49), and was defeated by Stephen A. Douglas in the U.S. Senate race for Illinois in 1858. Nationally, Lincoln had been a virtual political unknown until his engagement with Douglas on the slavery issue during the Illinois senatorial race in 1858. His brilliant address at New York City's Cooper Union in 1860 firmly solidified his presidential credentials on the slavery issue. His tall and lanky frame, ill-fitting suits and facial expression of sadness seemed to others as not such "as belongs to a handsome man."[3] A self-educated country lawyer whose political base was in Springfield, Lincoln cast his presidential prospects on the art of "compromise," the candidate who could be acceptable to all. Compromise was critical, especially as the 10,000 Republican party delegates assembled in the newly constructed Chicago convention hall known as the Wigwam came to the realization that principle contenders for the nomination, William Seward, Salmon Chase and Edwin Bates were not likely to receive the nomination. Both Seward and Chase had impressive anti-slavery credentials, but both men represented extremism. At a time when a more conciliatory approach was needed, both Seward and Chase advocated interference with slavery in places where it already existed as well as its prevention from spreading into new territories. Bates was associated with the Know Nothings and its accompanying anti-immigrant and anti-Catholic posture. Lincoln's floor managers at the convention waged a brilliant campaign to position their man as offering the best possible alternative to what was surely to emerge as a deadlock. From a national standpoint, Chase, Seward and Bates were simply unelectable. Lincoln won the nomination on the third ballot, after neither Seward nor any of the others failed to procure the needed number of delegates.[4] The election of Abraham Lincoln was perceived by the South as their worst nightmare come true. Following the election, South Carolina declared it was seceding from the Union on December 20th, 1860. Other slave states followed in rapid order including Mississippi, Florida, Alabama, Louisiana and Georgia. The purpose of these moves on the part of the seceding states was not merely to leave the United States but to establish a new country under the name of the *Confederate States of America*. The newly formed Confederacy organized a government and elected former United States Senator from Mississippi, Jefferson Davis, as its first President. While events moved beyond the ability of reasonable men to control, a fragile peace prevailed. Many leaders in the states of the upper south attempted to talk their brethren into reconsidering their action with respect to secession. President Buchanan feebly croaked out how secession was unconstitutional, but did little else in the remaining months of his term to avert the ominous drift of the country toward war. When Lincoln was finally inaugurated on March 4th, 1861, his address was conciliatory toward the South, stressing that it was not his intention to interfere with slavery where it already existed; however, with respect to future territory, Lincoln was adamant with respect to upholding the principles of "free soil." In short order, four more states seceded, and when Lincoln announced that the South was not going to be permitted to take over United States military facilities within its boundaries, the stage was set for armed confrontation.

Two forts guarded the approach to Charleston Harbor, Fort Sumter and Fort Moultrie. Fort Moultrie was under the command of regular army officer, Major Robert Anderson. On December 26th, 1860, Anderson secretly evacuated his garrison to the better and newer installation at Sumter. As Moultrie was more vulnerable, Sumter afforded defenders the benefit of a much stronger fortification. On January 9th, 1861, President Buchanan attempted to resupply Anderson's garrison by sending the unarmed merchant ship, *Star of the West*, into Charleston Harbor. The attempt failed when shore batteries opened up on the ship, preventing it from completing its mission. All Federal property in the Charleston area was subsequently declared forfeited to the Confederate States, that is, all the property except for Anderson's garrison at Sumter. On April 13th, after thirty-three hours of bombardment by Charleston shore batteries, the fort was surrendered to the Confederacy.[5]

The attack on Fort Sumter was the curtain rising event of the American Civil War. By the end of this four year national conflagration, almost 700,000 Americans would be dead. Rage and highly excited calls for action shot across the North as news of the attack spread. In thousands of villages and towns, war meetings were organized against a backdrop of fifes, drums and patriotically inflamed speeches.

Abraham Lincoln, in preparing to deal with the most consequential emergency in the nation's history to date, had already demonstrated a penchant for political genius high and above the abilities earlier perceived and ascribed to him by his former competitors. The backwoods circuit lawyer had assembled a cabinet unsurpassed in terms of political genius by installing not just one of his former political competitors, but all of them. The most significant and far reaching of these appointments was to be the conduit through which John Hughes, now Archbishop of New York, would move from a Catholic of national to international stature. That conduit was William Henry Seward.

II

In spite of the fierce blow of losing the nomination, there was palpable fear that Seward would not wholeheartedly support the party's nomination for president. Nonetheless, he committed himself to the success of the Republican ticket in November. Although he had considered resignation from the Senate in the immediate aftermath of his defeat, he wisely reasoned that to do so would appear the height of childishness. After a period of self-reflection and assessment, Seward joined the Republican campaign with renewed vigor. In every northern city and village, Seward was the central figure of the Republican drive for the Presidency. Any uneasiness in the minds of party operatives as to whether or not he along with Thurlow Weed were going to sit out the campaign, or worse, be so lackluster as to have no appreciable bearing on the possible outcome of the contest proved to be unfounded. Raised in spirit by the adulation still adoringly identified by his supporters as the true anti-slavery spokesman, "Old Irrepressible," as Seward was known, embarked on a western trip in the company of Massachusetts Congressman Charles Francis Adams. On the last day of August, 1860, Seward set out from Auburn on a speech making tour of five weeks in the states of Michigan, Wisconsin, Minnesota, Iowa, Missouri, Kansas, Illinois and Ohio. His notoriety was huge, with large crowds anxiously awaiting him at each railroad stop or boat landing to hear him speak. He was regarded as a great statesman,[6] even though his candidacy for president had been foiled by the brooding rail splitter from the West. In spite of having suffered such a humiliating defeat at the hands of a man Edwin Stanton had once described as a "baboon," Seward's old handler, Thurlow Weed, recognized the inherently sharp political aptitude of Lincoln. Lincoln knew Seward's support was going to be crucial in the campaign for the White House, and Seward, roused from the tempting inclination to succumb to self-pity, determined to be a vibrant force in that campaign. He stepped forward to speak on the vital issues facing the nation with a determination and urgency that provided the excitement of what was to be the most important Presidential race in the seventy-one years since the election of George Washington as the country's first President in 1789.

With Seward in the vanguard of the Republican campaign, he was greeted in a circus like atmosphere at the numerous stops he visited to campaign. Over 50,000 gathered to hear him in Detroit. On October 1st, Lincoln and Seward met in Springfield for the first time since meeting at a speaking engagement in Massachusetts in 1848. Although typical of American Presidential candidates of the time, Lincoln made no public statements, leaving that aspect to his surrogates. Lincoln focused his energies on holding together the coalition of old Democrats, former Whigs and members of the nativist American Party that had made his nomination possible.[7]

On Election Day, November 6th, 1860, Lincoln headed out to the courthouse in Springfield to cast his vote for President. Throughout the day, returns from the various sections of the country were pouring into local telegraph offices. Throughout the early part of the evening, Lincoln, with characteristic coolness and aplomb, waited out the returns with friends. By 9: 00 P.M. that evening, the returns from far off states were reflecting a successful result for Republicans, and by 11:30 P.M., the long awaited tally from the key state of New York revealed that steady gains had thus far been the order of the night. Still not completely settled, at least in Lincoln's mind, he cautioned his anxious friends and supporters, "Not too fast, my friends. Not too fast, it may not be over yet."[7]

As midnight approached, Lincoln attended a victory supper organized by the Republican ladies club. If he had doubts about the outcome, his fears were quickly allayed by reports that the Weed machine in New York had literally been rounding up every single Republican vote since morning. In the early hours of November 7th, Lincoln forces received confirmation that their man had been elected. By the time Lincoln retired to bed at around 2: 00 A.M., he realized how exhausted he was. Suddenly, the excitement and anticipation that had sustained him through the many months leading up to the convention, winning the nomination and ultimate victory in the general election now suddenly dissipated. While listening to the jubilant cries of his neighbors outside on the street, he started to feel the oppressive weight of the huge responsibility of the office he had just won. Though he shared the elation with his neighbors, he intuitively knew that such joy would never again be experienced. His craving for accomplishment and recognition was to play itself out on the bloodiest stage the world would ever witness, as he prepared himself to become the first and last American President to ever be called upon to hold together and preserve the United States.

From the start, Lincoln wisely determined that his main rival, William Seward, was to be marked for special distinction with respect to a cabinet post. Seward's ability, devoted service and unquestioned influence made him the ideal candidate for Secretary of State. The appointment, which was the *prima creatura* of the American Presidential Cabinet, was not only a thank you for ability, but for the vigorous campaign Seward had undertaken on behalf of Lincoln in the use of his influence in bringing New York State into the Lincoln column. The significance of confirmation of Seward at State was to be of far reaching consequence for not only the immediate necessity of bringing the Seward faction of the party firmly back into the fold, but also for the yet unseen and potentially perilous diplomatic landscape that was to emerge in European capitals, as the United States sank deeper and deeper into a bloody and factious civil war. There was no secret that England and continental European countries such as France, Spain and the Vatican harbored no great love for the United States. Through Seward, Lincoln was to make the acquaintance of Hughes, and ultimately utilize the feisty Catholic prelate in a most extraordinary mission to European heads of state for the purpose of promoting the cause of the Union. That such a mission would fall to Hughes was not surprising, as Hughes, more than any other American Catholic ecclesiastic figure was both widely known and respected, outspoken in his Americanism, and more importantly, anxious to show that his Irish people were ready to assume their share of the burden in the preservation of the adopted country Hughes loved. Lincoln would have great need of Hughes, who by virtue of stature and experience, would be able to act as an effective voice for the American cause overseas. Many of the Irish Catholics under Hughes's spiritual care were to be put to the test in fire and steel on battlefields with names like Antietam, Gettysburg and Cold Harbor. Hughes, while addressing the Hibernian Society of Charlestown, South on March 17th, 1860, eloquently articulated his love for the land of his birth: "Let the Irish people become educated, let them preserve the vigor of their national character and intellect, and they may bid defiance to the slang of pretended novel writers. Their position already entitles them to the admiration of impartial and enlightened minds throughout the world. I trust, therefore, you will agree with me in sentiment, which I am about to propose, as being the most appropriate to this festive occasion in commemoration of Ireland's patron saint. I propose, gentlemen, as a sentiment: The Land of the Shamrock. No one born within its borders need be ashamed of his birthplace."[8]

III

While the Hughes-Seward axis would soon be opened to the Lincoln administration, there was no mistaking the very strong views that John Hughes held with respect to the slavery question, one which he viewed as being of less importance than the more pressing reprehensible issue of secession and dissolution of the union. Hughes was no lover of abolitionism... "We Catholics, and a vast majority of our brave troops in the field, have not the slightest idea of carrying on a war that costs so much blood and treasure just to gratify a clique of Abolitionists."[9] That Hughes was an ardent opponent of secession was no more clearly articulated than in the voluminous correspondence with Catholic bishops of the South, one of whom was Patrick Nelson Lynch, Bishop of Charleston, South Carolina. Lynch was probably the most politically active Southern American

Catholic bishop during the Civil War. Born in Ireland in 1817, he was ordained to the priesthood in Rome in 1840. Invited to the United States by Bishop Reynolds to edit the *United States Catholic Miscellany,* he was named Bishop of the Diocese of Charleston in 1857. While friendly with Hughes, the two prelates were at opposite ends of the slavery issue as well as secession. Jefferson Davis would ask Nelson in 1864 to plead the cause of the Southern Confederacy to the Vatican – a mission which ultimately failed, leaving Lynch imprisoned in Rome until after the hostilities ended. Lynch was an articulate spokesman for the Southern cause. His exchanges with Hughes were always cordial, yet one could readily detect the sectional tension between the two men concerning the causes and possible effects of the conflict between North and South. Writing to Lynch on May 7th, 1861, Hughes made the argument with respect to the "principles" involved in the North's decision to go to war and its implications for Catholics: "With regard to Catholics, North and South, I can have but little to say. I myself have never recommended any man to go to war, unless circumstances rendered it expedient or necessary... deprecating the assumed necessity for this war. I have not interfered by giving them advice to do so. It is the same with the South, I presume. But certainly there is a great difference in principle between the two sections of the country. The North have not been required to do anything new, to take an oath, support any new flag; they have kept on the even tenor of their way. The South, on the contrary, has taken upon itself to be the judge in its own cause, to be witness in its own cause, and to execute, if necessary, by force of arms, its own decision. In a constitutional country, this means either revolution or rebellion, since there are tribunals agreed upon North or South, supported by both for a period of more than seventy years."[10]

Writing on August 4th, 1861, Lynch recapitulated the events that not only led to the crisis of division between North and South, but the inevitable consequences following the decision of the North to force a war upon the South: "Well, South Carolina seceded – other states were preparing to follow her. The matter was taken up in Congress. Many southerners hoped that then, when the seriousness of the questions could no longer be doubted, something might be done. How vainly they hoped, the Committees of Congress showed. The alternative was thus forced on the South either of tame submission or resistance. They did not hesitate. They desired to withdraw in peace. This war has been forced upon them. It was necessary in the beginning. It brings ruins to thousands in its prosecution. It will be fruitless of any good. At the conclusion, the parties will stand apart exhausted and embittered by it; for every battle, however, won or lost, will have served to have widened the chasm between the North and the South, and to render more difficult, if not impossible, any future reconstruction. Will it be a long war, or a short and mighty one? The cabinet and northern press have pronounced for the last. Yet this is little more than an idle dream...."[11]

Hughes abhorred abolition in all of its extremities, and most importantly, its hypocrisy. Many abolitionists who espoused the cause of the Negro in the high tone language of Christian morality were not equally enthusiastic about espousing the cause of social justice for the hundreds of thousands of desperately poor Catholic Irish immigrants, struggling to gain a foothold on the lowest rung of American society. Many noted abolitionists were professed nativist bigots. The inconsistency that rankled Hughes more than the moral hollowness of abolition was the fact that many abolitionists could neither concede nor imagine a society where freed Negroes could ever hope to be fully accepted or viewed as equal to whites. Hughes was also a practical man. While he did strongly advocate decent treatment for those enslaved, he firmly believed that massive numbers of freed slaves would further challenge the opportunities of his own Irish immigrants, who clearly in the period from their arrival in the mid 1840s until the outbreak of hostilities between North and South were among the most economically de- pressed group ever to arrive on America's shores. Allegations were often raised by militant Northern Protestants that Hughes, because of his known antipathy toward abolition, was pro-secession and anti-Union. It was only natural for those who held this position to progress to the next step of assuming that the legions of Irish Catholics could neither be counted on nor trusted to become good, loyal, Union support-ing Americans – Americans prepared to give their allegiance to the President of the United States rather than a foreign Pope. To the contrary, Hughes, by the time of Fort Sumter's surrender, had already emerged as an ardent pro-American and pro-Union defender. In cities, towns and villages all across the country, war meetings were organized against the martial strain of marching bands. The call to arms through-out the North had reached a fever pitch. As everywhere, men denounced the attack by South Carolina secessionists on a military installation of the United States. In New York City, a massive war rally was held in Union Square on April 21st, 1861. Over 100,000 persons jammed into the square amidst banners, streamers and fiery anti-Southern speeches. Not-ables such as John A. Dix, Fernando Wood and William F. Havemeyer stepped up to the rostrum to denounce the South's wanton aggression as well as introduce a variety of war related resolutions. Although not able to be present at the rally, a letter penned by Archbishop John Hughes was read out to the assembled multitude: "Unable to attend the meeting at Union Square, in consequence of indisposition, I beg to have my sentiments on the subject of your coming together in the following words: ministers of religion and minsters of peace, according to the instruction of their Divine master, are not ceased to hope and pray that peace and union may be preserved in his great and free country. At present however, that question has been taken out of the hands of the peacemakers and it is referred to the arbitra-ment of a sanguinary contest. I am not authorized to speak in the name of my fellow citizens. I think as far as I can judge, there is the right principle all among them, who I know, it is now thirty years since, a foreigner by birth, I took the oath of allegiance to this country, under its title of the United States of America." {Loud Cheers}... "In reference to my duties as citizen, no change has come over my mind since then. The Government of the United States was then, and it is now, symbolized by the national flag, popularly called the Stars and Stripes {Loud Applause} This has been my flag and shall be to the end.{Cheers} I trust it is still destined to display in the gales that sweep every ocean, and amid the gentle breezes of many a distant shore, as I have seen it in foreign lands, its own peculiar waving lines of beauty, whether at home or abroad, for a thousand years, and afterwards as long as Heaven permits, without limit or duration."[12]

Irish Americans embraced the opportunity to demonstrate their loyalty to the cause of the Union by enlisting in the ranks of the National Army. More than 140,000 men of Irish blood joined in the fight against the South. Nearly one third of these active enlistments came from New York City, and of this number, none was more famous than the Irish Brigade. Authorized by Secretary of War Simon Cameron in 1861, the brigade consisted of the 69th New York Infantry, the 63rd New York Infantry and the 88th New York Infantry Regiments. A fourth regiment consisting of mostly nativist Yankee troops of the 29th Massachusetts Regiment was never enamored of being incorporated into a fighting outfit with Irish troops and after the Battle of Antietam, was dropped in place of the 28th Massachusetts Regiment, one which incorporated more native born Irishmen. The 116th Pennsylvania Infantry regiment was later added to round out the Brigade. Although many regiments ultimately answered the clarion call to arms in New York, it was the Irish Brigade that came to symbolize the participation of the immigrant Irish in the struggle to preserve the United States. On April 23rd, 1861, the Brigade was given a rousing send-off as it made its way along Prince Street in New York, past the Cathedral of Old St. Patrick's, before turning South onto Mott Street, headed toward its point of embarkation for Washington. Upon arrival in the nation's capital, it once again received a festive and enthusiastic reception. In its first engagement during the opening battle of the Civil War on July 25th, 1861 at Bull Run, Virginia, the brigade made a creditable stance and held its position on the field until ordered to withdraw. When finally ordered to pull back, it did so in an orderly fashion. Even with heavy losses of 39 killed on that fateful day and its commanding officer, Colonel Corcoran, a captive of the Confederates, the Irish brigade would go on to achieve glory and fame on many more hotly contested battlefields of the American Civil War, including Antietam, Gettysburg and Cold Harbor.

While patriotic feeling ran high, the many soldiers killed in battle had a profound effect on the Irish American community of New York City. Increased relief efforts were directed toward the soldiers at the front. The Friendly Sons of St. Patrick raised the substantial amount of $1,500.00 to defray the cost of equipment and medical supplies for the Irish soldiers. Families, who had lost a bread winner in the fighting, were cared for by the diligent and generous relief committees organized for the purpose of providing monetary support. By May of 1861, several thousands of dollars had been raised with the promise that support would continue for as long as the troops had to remain in the field.[13] Mass Irish meetings, such as the one held in Jones Wood (present day Sixty-sixth to Seventy-fifth Streets from Third Avenue to the East River) on August 29th, 1861, resulted in the largest assembly of financial contributions ($60,000.00) toward providing relief for the widows and orphans of those who had fallen in battle.

In the early stages of the War, enlistments typically expired after ninety days, but with the unforeseen casualties and carnage of Bull Run now etched into the minds of military men both North and South, the country was starting to acknowledge that it was going to be a long and bloody conflict. In spite of this grim reality, reenlistments among the Irish outfits seemed to be high, as men appeared willing and ready to rejoin the fight. It would take that caliber of commitment, as the easy days of camp life and parade field marches were quickly giving way to the harsh and brutal reality of a hot war, with shots fired in anger for the purpose of killing the "enemy."

An editorial in *The Irish American* called for the formation of a single, massive Irish fighting force, no doubt calling to mind the glory of the Irish brigades that fought on the continent of Europe in service to the monarchs of every nation but their own. Initially, Hughes had found the idea appealing; however, the concentration of any large number of ethnic fighters in a large force, whether Irish, or German or anything else could pose potential problems before the enemy ever came into sight. The Irish troops possessed a unique bond in their Catholic faith. Just as during the War with Mexico, Hughes was very much concerned that sufficient numbers of Catholic chaplains be available to accompany soldiers into combat. As the spiritual leaders of the Irish Catholic community, Catholic priests would serve as the protectors not only of the Faith and Sacraments, but function as administrators of the general welfare for the soldiers. In addition to celebrating the Sacrifice of the Mass, hearing confessions and administering the last rights, Catholic chaplains would serve in the same capacity they did amongst the Irish in peace time, that is, as advocates of sobriety, good morals, religious devotion and perhaps of equally great importance, the proper use of pay to care for families. At times chaplains acted as bankers and even took over a soldier's individual savings to insure that monies were regularly set aside to provide for one's dependents.[14]

Prejudice against Irish Catholics had historically run a deep current in the United States Army, especially among the officer corps. Largely because of the tremendous influence of Secretary Seward, Lincoln came more and more to know and rely on John Hughes for advice, especially with respect to Catholic issues, which Lincoln would have had scant understanding or familiarity with. Lincoln was not disposed to the wild and inflammatory anti-Catholic rhetoric that permeated much of the talk and thinking of his political contemporaries. To the contrary, Lincoln, even then, recognized the potential importance of the Irish both in terms of his War as well as political objectives. With great diplomatic deference, Lincoln, in a letter to Hughes dated October 21st, 1861 made inquiries with respect to the appointment of Catholic hospital chaplains for the Union Army: "I am sure you will pardon me, if in my ignorance, I do not address with technical correctness. I find no law authorizing the appointment of chaplains for our hospitals; and yet the services of chaplains are more needed, perhaps, in the hospitals, than with the healthy soldiers in the field. With this view, I have given a sort of quasi appointment (a copy of which I enclose) to each of three protestant ministers, who have accepted and entered upon their duties. If you perceive no objection,

I will thank you to give the names of one or two more suitable persons of the Catholic Church, to whom I may properly with propriety, tender the same service. Many thanks for your kind and judicious letters to Gov. Seward, which he regularly allows me both the pleasure and profit of seeing."[15]

The Union military effort in the first two years of the conflict was largely unsuccessful in comparison to the Confederacy. The Lincoln Administration initially suffered from a lack of solid military leadership. With the outbreak of hostilities in 1861, massive resignations of regular army officers, many of whom were southern and loyal to their respective states, Robert, E. Lee, J.E.B Stuart, Lewis Armistead, P.G.T. Beauregard and Thomas Jonathan "Stonewall" Jackson, to name but a few, greatly handicapped the Northern war effort in the field. Just as in peace time, Lincoln was bedeviled by having to make "political" appointments, the only difference being that many appointments of men to the rank of general was oftentimes less about ability than fulfillment of some political expedient. But perhaps no greater impediment to the early war effort came from Lincoln's first important commanding general, George B. McClellan.

George Brinton McClellan was born in Philadelphia, Pennsylvania in 1826 and graduated from the United States Military Academy at West Point in 1846, distinguishing himself during the War with Mexico (1846-1848). McClellan left the army in 1857 to pursue career interests in the railroad industry, but returned to volunteer his services at the outbreak of hostilities after the surrender of Fort Sumter. Because the emerging Union army was larger, more complex and greatly in need of experienced officers more than at any time since the beginning of the nation's history, it became a time of unparalleled opportunity and advancement for someone with McClellan's prior military training and accomplishments. Promoted to the rank of major-general, McClellan, or "Little Mac" as he was to be known, was responsible for the training and formation of the early recruits pouring into Washington, D.C. It was said of McClellan that he was a man capable of "strutting" while sitting down. Short in stature and regal in military bearing,

he quickly became the idol of the green troops slowly
evolving into the formidable fighting force that was to
become the Army of the Potomac. McClellan's meticulous
attention to planning and detail was to emerge as the chief
undoing of his ability to challenge opponents to a decisive
engagement on the battlefield. He had a penchant for consistently over estimating the size and strength of his
opponent as well as a tendency to leave substantial numbers
of his troops unengaged at decisive points during a military
action. His timidity and petulance was a source of endless
irritation to Lincoln, who on three occasions relieved
McClellan of command, replacing him with men of even
lesser capability and, disillusioned, forced to restoring
McClellan to command again. On the diplomatic front, the
Union effort was progressing little better than on the military
one. England had greatly benefited from the Southern cotton
trade, so there was no surprise that the English were hoping
for a Confederate victory. Aside from purely economic considerations, other European powers watched the unfolding
events in America with a disdainful satisfaction. The French
and Spanish salivated not only at the prospect of seeing the
upstart American democratic experiment fail but also for
repossession of lost land and influence. Lincoln knew that
continued failure to produce a credible battlefield victory for
the North might somehow embolden some of the European
powers to recognize the Confederacy. Lincoln, realizing the
disastrous potential of such a development, turned to the
one man, who by virtue of his standing not only in the
Vatican but the capitals of Europe, was in a position to be
an advocate for the cause of the Union. Lincoln determined
to have Hughes embark on a diplomatic mission to Ireland,
England, France, Spain and Italy for the purpose of arguing
the cause of the Union. When this mission was first broach-
ed by Seward, Hughes, quite naturally was reluctant to
accede to the request. Much hung in the balance on this
most critical mission; still, it was an assignment that could
not be cast aside. Agreeing to undertake the journey, with
Thurlow Weed acting as his secretary, Hughes embarked
upon this most critical diplomatic journey.

Hughes's departure was timely, as an international incident further exacerbated the relationship of a divided United States with England. Two Southern agents, James Mason and John Slidell, had boarded the British steamship Trent bound for England for the avowed purpose of seeking recognition of the Confederacy. The U.S.S. Jacinta, under the command of Captain John Wilkes, intercepted the Trent and placed both Mason and Slidell under arrest. Wilkes was immediately hailed as a hero in the North; however, in England, his actions were condemned and viewed as an act of war against a sovereign nation. England prepared for war.[15] Largely due to the skill of American British Ambassador John Francis Adams and Queen Victoria's consort, Prince Albert, tempers were cooled and the British Ambassador in Washington presented his protest over the incident tactfully.

In Ireland, Hughes took the opportunity to address a gathering of lay and churchmen on the occasion of the opening of Catholic University in Dublin: "Gentlemen, I will not say a word of America. I suppose I know as well as if I were born there, perhaps better, that there may be found there the weaknesses, passions, and prejudices that are more or less the effect of mankind. I don't advise a single countryman of mine to go there if he can do well at home; still, I would say in the presence of these venerable prelates and these devoted clergy who have consecrated their lives, I might say for the protection and salvation of their flocks... I would say to them, send us none who are drunkards, none who are bound up with secret societies in this, your land, whether Orangemen or Ribbonmen; give us good men, and now is particularly the time for them; men who will do honor to their country."[16]

Critics would point to words like this as a hardly veiled attempt on the part of Hughes to recruit Irishmen into the ranks of the Union Army, when in fact, no proof of any such activity could ever be shown to exist. So long as Erin's sons sought out America's shores for refuge from economic and religious persecution, Hughes was merely expressing a fervent hope that they would prove to be men of good morals and character, attributes requisite for the building of strong nations. Continuing on this same theme in an address to the

Catholic Young Men's Society during the same visit, Hughes focused on the needed traits for success in Ireland and America: "I thought I should meet with *The Catholic Young Men's Society*, to congratulate them upon the good which I have been told they are doing, sustaining each other in piety and perseverance. I had no other purpose or object in view than to say to them a few words of encouragement. I intended to tell them how their countrymen in America, of the same professions, occupations and conditions in life, also labored in works of this kind; and I wish to encourage them in that way... To tell them that young Irishmen coming to America, if they are well inclined, if they are sober, but above all, if they are unshackled by those... I would call them infernal bonds... secret societies; if they keep clear of these things, there is reasonable chance for success for them in America."[17]

IV

Accepting of Lincoln's invitation to act as a diplomatic agent on behalf of the Union was not one easily acceded too by Hughes. No doubt recalling his encounter with President Polk and the intrigue that surrounded his consideration as an unofficial emissary to meet with the Mexican government, Hughes was sensitive to possible charges of the Lincoln Administration acting in league with the Pope. While the strident anti-Catholicism of the period had somewhat been ameliorated by the substantial response of Irish Catholics to fight for and defend the Union, the embers of religious bigotry were never far from reigniting. Lincoln, ever mindful of the potential firestorm that might result in utilizing someone like Hughes in so sensitive a position, was convinced that the American cause would have no better advocate in the courts of Europe. Still, the departure of Hughes and Thurlow Weed was a low keyed affair, and *Harper's Weekly* on November 23rd, 1861 reported "that Mr. Weed and Archbishop Hughes left this port [New York] on Saturday last for Europe. He states himself that he goes on private business;

the public, however, will be apt to suspect that his private business concerns the public interest. If the suspicion be correct, we may feel assured that our affairs will suffer no mischance in his hands. Few men in the country are such true patriots as Thurlow Weed."[18]

Good will and intentions aside, both men were to be confronted with a prickly political landscape once they arrived on the other side of the Atlantic. It cannot be overstated how critical the Hughes mission for the Lincoln Administration was, as recognition of the Confederacy could have proven fatal for the continued prospect of survival for the American nation. European leaders felt threatened by a strong, unified America. They had no qualms in expressing the desire to see a divided country, a country whose diminished power would ultimately mean greater security and safety for Europe. Europe, even then, believed that American ambition had to be thwarted by supporting the subdivision of a single unified entity into smaller and less influential states. Upon arrival on the continent, Weed headed to London to engage in discussions with members of Queen Victoria's government and Hughes, after a brief stay in Ireland, departed for France to see Napoleon III.

When Hughes arrived in France, he immediately was forced to deal with another problem, one that was the exclusive creation of the official diplomatic representative of his own government. U.S. Minister to Paris, Thomas Drayton, proved uncooperative and not anxious to help someone whose status was merely that of an unofficial agent. He refused to arrange for Hughes to meet with Napoleon and Empress Eugenie. Hughes had a critical decision to make; news of the arrest of Slidell and Mason had taken place almost simultaneously with his arrival in France, and so it was therefore necessary to meet with the French monarchs to preempt any possible negative effect on public opinion. One of the principle hurdles that Hughes had to overcome with the French was their belief that an independent Confederacy would provide a needed buffer between royalist Mexico and the republican United States. Since the install-ment of Maximillian, the younger brother of Austrian Emperor Franz Joseph I as part of the joint French and

Austrian plan to invade, conquer and rule Mexico in 1861, Napoleon III was seeking to legitimize French claims to rule Mexico for France. Supported by the French army and pro Mexican monarchists opposed to the administration of liberal President Benito Juarez, Maximillian would ultimately travel to Mexico for the purpose of setting up his puppet regime. The French intervention in Mexico was in direct violation of the Monroe Doctrine, but Lincoln was acutely aware of the tight rope he needed to walk to avoid conflict not only with England, but France as well. The United States in 1861 was not in a position to court armed conflict with two major European powers. Hughes was skillful in his discussions with Napoleon, making him believe that should war breakout between the United States and England, French influence could be brought to bear with respect to mediation. Additionally, Hughes also raised the prospect of French development of Algeria as an alternative cotton market. Finally, in a stroke of diplomatic genius, Hughes successfully raised the ire of the Empress Eugenie, a Spaniard, regarding the American naval blockade of Cuba by strongly emphasizing the Confederate intention of converting the island into an extension of the evil Southern empire of slavery.[19]

Hughes had scored a great personal rather than diplomatic victory with the French. While Napoleon gave no assurance to the prelate regarding French intentions, Hughes came away from the exchange believing France to be generally more favorably disposed to the Union cause than originally believed. Recognition of the Confederacy was not forthcoming from France, and the Emperor's address to the *Corps Legislatif* was ultimately a friendlier one in tone and content.

Arriving in Rome, while Hughes basked in and was the recipient of the Pope's favor, he still had to complete a very specific mission. Hughes appealed to the Pope to keep the Vatican out of the conflict despite the intensive pressure being exerted by Confederate States President, Jefferson Davis. The South had dispatched its own Catholic official in the person Bishop Patrick Lynch of the Diocese of Charleston and, later on, Father John Bannon, for the purpose of

pleading the cause of the Confederacy. Here again the stature and regard for Hughes kept the Pontiff neutral. In his
many meetings with both pilgrims as well as high ecclesiastic
officials, Hughes promoted the American position and, as
with the Empress Eugenie, raised concern among Spanish
bishops with respect to the dubious intentions of the South
concerning expansion of slavery in Cuba.

The Hughes mission was of incalculable importance to
the survival of the United States during a most critical
period in its history. Torn asunder by civil war, America
found itself without many friends overseas. Returning to the
United States from his diplomatic mission in late 1862,
Hughes, in a letter to Seward, summarized in painfully acute
detail the state of anti-Americanism than in existence: "On
the other hand, I may say that no day – no hour even – was
spent in Europe in which I did not, according to opportunity,
labor for peace between Europe and America. So far, that
peace has not been disturbed. But let America be prepared.
There is no love for the United States on the other side of the
Atlantic, the United States are ignored, if not despised;
treated in conversation in the same contemptuous language
as we might employ toward the inhabitants of the Sandwich
Islands, or Washington Territory, or Vancouver island, or the
settlement of the Red River or of the Hudson Bay's Territory.
This may be considered very unpolished, almost unchristian
language proceeding from the pen of a Catholic Archbishop.
But, my dear Governor, it is unquestionably true, and I am
sorry to say that it is so. If you, in Washington, are not able
to defend yourselves in case of need, I do not see where or
from what source you can expect friendship or protection."

Proof of this contention was further demonstrated when
an official request from a grateful Lincoln Administration to
have Hughes raised to the dignity of the office of Cardinal
was diplomatically turned aside by the Vatican. Even though
Hughes had managed to keep the scale balanced during this
critical early period of the Civil War, there still existed,
especially within the hallowed precincts of the Roman Curia,
a hardy veiled contempt of America and its liberal experiment in representative democracy. Though Hughes most
likely was the closest he was ever to be for consideration of

so great an accolade as the Cardinal's Red Hat, such a request coming from the head of state of a nation of heretical, Protestant and republican beliefs was doomed to rejection.

The strenuous overseas mission, which had kept Hughes out of his New York Archdiocese for well over a year, had taken a definite toll physically on the aging and ailing prelate. Writing to the Reverend Father Bernard Smith on October 16th, 1862, Hughes reflected that "You can imagine the accumulation of business of every description that had taken place during my absence, which none but myself could dispose of. I have been able to get through this to every great extent; but still, neither can I enjoy for the present, nor even look forward to enjoying in the future, that kind of repose and leisure which many bishops in Europe are familiar."[20]

Again writing to Smith on December 15th, Hughes alluded to concerns over his steadily deteriorating health, no doubt from years of stress related ailments, erratic eating habits and increasing bouts of rheumatism. "I have had, from the middle of October, an attack more serious as usual. Its origin, I think, was from my preaching in the open air, and administering the sacrament of confirmation to some four or five hundred Catholic soldiers who were preparing to, in Camp Scott, Staten Island, for the coming struggle of battle."[21]

After completion of a service that by anyone's standard represented patriotic devotion to the country, Hughes again found himself immersed in controversy, this time however, not with heads of state, but with co-religionists in his own country.

Almost immediately after Hughes returned to New York, he preached a great sermon to the people of the city about his overseas journey and mission. He spoke of the purpose of his visit to so many foreign capitals on behalf of the United States, and urged the American people to mentally and physically pull together for the purpose of prosecuting the war to its conclusion. In the Same address he also vigorously praised President Lincoln's recent call for the drafting of hundreds of thousands new men to take up the fight: "If I had a voice in the councils of the country, I would say let the volunteering continue; if three hundred on your list not be enough this week, make as draft of three hundred thousand more. It is not cruel, this. This is mercy; this is humanity. Anything that will put an end to this drenching of blood the whole surface of the country that will be human-ity... it is not necessary to hate our enemies. It is not necessary to be cruel in battle, nor to be cruel after its termination. It is necessary to be true, to be patriotic, to do for the country what the country needs, and the blessing of God will recompense those who discharge their duty without faltering, and without violating any of the laws of God or man."[22]

Hughes's endorsement of Lincoln's call for a draft was received with coolness by Catholic clerics in the South. Additionally, the same group found it distasteful that Hughes had in effect allowed himself to be used as a quasi-envoy for Abraham Lincoln. The focal point of the criticism came from Baltimore, a slave city with a long history of Pro-Southern sentiment. The attacks against Hughes came from the *The Catholic Mirror,* who excoriated Hughes for promoting aggres-sion against the South by support of a draft. In some Southern Catholic quarters, it was felt that "during this sad contest the Catholic clergy, at least, would have kept their skirts clean of blood."[23]

The Hughes contribution to preserving the Union was without qualification one of the major diplomatic accomplish-ments of Abraham Lincoln. Through Hughes, a most delicate balance was maintained between the intense and bitterly rivaled interests of the United States and Europe, even though in the end, failure of a major European power to give an outright endorsement to the Confederacy was perhaps predicated more on hard headed political considerations than the efforts of an American Catholic bishop. This reality was succinctly stated by England's Prince Albert, consort of Queen Victoria, who mused about what would happen if England had opted to go to war against a bitterly divided United States in the wake of the Mason-Slidell incident: "What are we going to have, Northern States and Southern States?"[24]

Whatever the state of real politik, the contribution of John Hughes to the war effort on behalf of his country was incalculable. As a Roman Catholic Churchman, he was the first to give service of this kind to the civilian government of the United States, a government heretofore less than accepting not only of John Hughes's Church, but of its Irish immigrant members.

Chapter 9

The Lion's Legacy

Assessing the Hughes legacy is a perilous undertaking, not so much because of who he was, but rather, because of what he was. As the child of a persecuted country, he was born into an era when a Roman Catholic's life in Ireland, under English law, hardly differed in many ways from the African slave working in a Mississippi or South Carolina field. As a man of poverty, all of his life's accomplishments, especially in the realm of getting an education, were accomplished through sheer will and perseverance. He came of age in America as a promising young cleric at a time when Catholicism was suffering the dual effects of severe growing pains as well as persistent and oftentimes violent persecution. For Hughes, once committed to achieving a goal, there was no amount of human endeavor that could be set against its ultimate success. His single minded persistence in pursuit of aims or to right an injustice often times propelled him along a collision course with the forces of political exclusion and prejudice. The memories of his own bitter experiences in Ireland, the uncompromising devotion to achieving his goal of becoming a priest and his open and intellectually challenging dialogue about Catholicism with some of its most virulent haters characterized the mettle of a man destined to become one of the American Catholic Church's most esteemed leaders. Against a backdrop of socially acceptable religious bigotry, violently acted out against Catholics more times than not, the appearance of John Hughes on the ecclesiastical scene marked that rare instance in American history where the dynamic forces of "personality" and "people" combine to foster a radical change of landscape. In the Revolutionary War generation, it was the magnetism of George Washington and the undying devotion accorded him as America's *pater noster*. Through him, America not only forged its way to military victory against Britain, but once established, looked to his firm hand and reputation for the leadership to guide a new nation through its tenuous, initial years. In Andrew Jackson, the "people" were to have a president whose hand was firmly planted on the tiller of those who elected him, rather than on the evil cadre of special interests. Similarly, Jackson was the first to hold the office believing that the president should be the spokesperson and representative of the ordinary man. In John Hughes was to be found a blend of both men. He was to emerge as a religious leader adored by his constituency, a destitute and reviled group of immigrants fleeing hunger and annihilation from the ravages of famine in their native Ireland. These Catholic immigrants were to become the touchstone of nativist and anti-Catholic discrimination and prejudice. Hughes would not only shepherd his people into assimilating into an unwelcoming American society, but would be a principle agent in the regeneration not only of their lost Catholic Faith but of the transformation of Roman Catholicism in America from a "closet" religious experience to its position as one of, if not the most influential and powerful institution within American society.

Hughes was to unapologetically take the new, raw material of the infant Catholic Church, immigrants from his native Ireland, and proceed to build an urban-based ecclesiastical organization whose head would never again be lowered in shame before nativist American bigots. By rekindling of the "Catholic" flame, Hughes was simultaneously preparing his people for political empowerment in a society that was openly hostile. His aggressive approach in carrying out this program was more of necessity than choice, as the age in which Hughes ascended to the episcopacy was characterized by the torch. While Catholic institutions in Boston, Philadelphia and other larger centers had been burnt to the ground, no such incidents occurred in New York, where in the face of credible threats, Hughes made it unequivocally clear that a violent act would be countered with a violent response. On more than one occasion, the Cathedral Church of the New York Diocese, which extended along Prince Street between Mott and Mulberry Streets, was lined with armed defenders specifically to turn any attempt at destruction of the building. Even the most rabid church burners grew in wariness of Hughes, and they had no doubt that Hughes would have been as good as his word in putting up a fight to defend the Faith. In facing the harsh realities of life for Catholics, especially those who were of Irish origin, Hughes sought to keep his flock intact. Not all Irish immigrants remained at the gates of their first urban port of entry in America. Some made it out into the hinterland, where eventual acquisition of a small tract of land might provide some semblance of the life they had left behind in Ireland. For those however who never made it beyond the teeming slums, Hughes believed it better to try and raise up and improve his people who, though poor, still had the moral support of fellow immigrants, churches and priests near at hand. This combination enabled many Irish immigrants to go from survival to launching a better way of life. Aggressive and autocratic traits aside, Hughes was in the process of accomplishing something for the Catholic Church in America that was not conceivable a generation before, no less becoming a reality. He was the American "nationalist," preaching not only the Gospel of Jesus Christ, but one of sobriety, good living and loyalty to the newly adopted land of his people. He had achieved celebrity and standing amongst American political figures of both parties, and was frequently consulted by key members of both. The regard that had been steadily growing for Hughes was beginning to have a positive effect for other Catholic prelates as well. So much had the esteem Hughes received during his lifetime been registered by the civilian government that President Andrew Johnson decided that it would be a good idea to stop in at the closing session of the Council of American Bishops in Baltimore in 1866. For

Hughes, leading his Church and his people over the threshold of acceptance and power was neither an easy task nor one readily acceded to by foes. He was a dictatorial leader, who brooked no dissent. The alternative was timidity and silence, and nothing in the makeup or history of John Hughes the person could have ever accommodated such dispositions.

I

The Irish were not the only significant Catholic population in New York City in need of spiritual attention and guidance. The sizable German population, along with French, Spanish and African American Catholics represented a substantial number of co-religionists next to the Irish, and were all but ignored by Hughes. It seemed as if these communities weren't paid much attention, or worse, not even considered to exist. The German Catholic population of New York differed greatly from their Irish counterparts. Firstly, the German Catholics who immigrated to America "went less to build something new, as opposed to regain and conserve something old."[1] Parish life was already an established facet of German religious life, and the German language was the preferred medium of communication. The retention of German was a principle factor in the creation of strong "National Parishes" within the German-American community. While no strangers to the debilitating effects of poverty existing within small pockets of the community, German Catholics generally were not associated with the widespread economic distress so prevalent within the Irish community. Hughes was largely indifferent to German Catholics, largely focusing the full measure of his outreach effort toward his own people. He seldom involved himself in their affairs, believing them to exhibit too narrow a national feeling and, as a result, found it tedious in attempting to satisfy their needs. Hughes was happy to delegate this business to his German Vicar General, John Raffeiner.[2] Born in 1785 in the Austrian Tyrol, Raffeiner had studied for the priesthood at the Tyrolean Benedictine Abbey in Fiecht and later in Rome. He had also trained in medicine, and before completing his theological studies in 1825, had practiced medicine and surgery in Italy, Austria and Switzerland. In response to an appeal by Bishop Edward Fenwick, Raffeiner volunteered to do missionary work in the United States. Fortunately, he proved an able administrator for Hughes, who never really succeeded in bridging the gap separating him from the German Catholics of his diocese.

Trouble with the Germans was only one of many difficulties experienced by Hughes during his period of episcopal reign, for it could hardly be said that it was a period of political tranquility and calm for New York. With Hughes so often in the eye of the storm in the continuous battles with nativist newspaper editors and Catholic detractors in general, battles over the proper place of parish trustees; Catholic school funding; Irish nationalist organizations and the proper place of religion in a democracy, there was plenty of fuel to stoke the flames of discord that prevailed during the Hughes tenure. Hughes himself was capable of tremendous obstinacy and stubbornness. He could be rigidly authoritarian. A Jesuit superior at Fordham with whom he quarreled stated that Hughes "had an extraordinarily overbearing character; he has to dominate."[3] Similarly, a trustee of old St. Patrick's Cathedral made no attempt to mask his desire to "horsewhip the bishop if he showed his face."[4] Again, Hughes was fortunate in being surrounded by those whose personality strengths made up for many of the prelate's lacking attributes. One such person was his extremely popular, cosmopolitan and conciliatory Vicar General of both the Diocese and Archdiocese, Father Felix Varela. Felix Varela y Morales was born in Havana, Cuba in 1788 at a time when Spain's overseas empire included not only the West Indies, but Louisiana, Florida and much what was then South America. His father had served as an officer in a Spanish regiment and from a young age, Felix demonstrated a strong inclination to pursue the priesthood.

Educated at the College and Seminary of San Jose, Varela was ordained in 1811. With the reinstitution of the Cortes (Spanish Parliament), Father Varela and two other men were selected to represent the island of Cuba in Madrid.

A fierce opponent of slavery, Varela had presented a detailed plan to the parliament proposing an end to slavery in Cuba without doing economic harm to the white population. The Holy Alliance, the compact of European monarchs who opposed the philosophy of social progress, forced Varela into exile. Arriving in America, he settled first in Philadelphia and then later in New York, where he continued to be outspoken against slavery and a forceful advocate for social justice. Invited by Bishop John Connolly, Varela was attached to the Church of St. Peter's on Barclay Street in lower Manhattan. The only other Catholic Church in New York at the time was St. Patrick's on Mulberry Street. As New York was a robustly growing immigrant Church, Varela's full energies were released in the missionary outreach work to the growing number of poor immigrants flooding the city. When Connolly's replacement, Jean DuBois, succeeded as New York's Diocesan Bishop, Varela proved to be an invaluable assistant to DuBois. DuBois's appointment precipitated fierce resentment on the part of the growing number of Irish Catholics. DuBois, the French-born aristocrat, had been appointed over their choice of John Power. Varela deftly maneuvered the trying task of ameliorating animosities of both the people as well as many clergy during DuBois's administration. Varela possessed a soothing touch, and brought a dignity and quiet strength to efforts at minimizing tensions. So impressed was DuBois with his Cuban priest, that he named him Vicar general of the Diocese in 1837, a post he would hold until 1853.[5] If John Hughes was characterized as the iron fist, then Varela was the velvet glove covering that fist. Massive waves of Irish immigrants who were destitute, unchurched and unschooled would require a more forceful approach then the salve of Varela diplomacy. Hughes entertained no false hope about the herculean task which he confronted relative to the famine survivors. A strict, disciplined and totalitarian approach was called for and just as in any loving family, child was bound to have broiling disagreements with parent. Such was the case with Hughes and his Irish people. No issue more clearly demonstrated this internal conflict than the emergence of militant Irish nationalism, resurrected in the wake of the revolutions that swept across the European continent in 1848. New York's immigrant Irish community came to reflect the bitterly strident divisions that existed within the nationalist movement in Ireland. Every group had its supporters, advocates and publications. Every group was represented within parish churches, benevolent societies and news outlets. While there was no doubt that John Hughes was an ardent supporter of Irish freedom, he preached a different revolutionary path: assimilation and loyalty to the United States. He avowedly hated participation in secret societies, the underbelly of what he believed to be the hallmark of failed Irish revolutionary activity. To Hughes, many of the Young Irelanders[6] had been tainted with irreligion, corrupted by French radicalism. One of the principle targets of Hughes's wrath was Thomas D'Arcy McGee of the Irish publication, *Nation.* McGee had made the sweeping charge that priests and bishops had been the primary reason for the failure of the 1848 rebellion in Ireland. Responding to the accusation in the *Freeman's Journal,* Hughes said,

> "The clergy would have been faithless to the obligations of religion and humanity, if they had not interposed, seeing as they must have seen the certain and inevitable consequence of a movement so nobly conceived, but so miserably conducted."[7]

For Hughes, the Church was key, and Hughes did everything in his power to focus that Church on the needs of the Irish masses in the spiritual realm, as well as the critical temporal needs of schools, hospitals, parishes and the practice of sound Catholic religious doctrine. Due to the tightly knit urban setting of Irish Americans in New York, it was assured that the Irish would eventually begin to flex their muscle in demanding proper recognition and place.

As a strong defender of the Union, he zealously opposed the Southern rebellion. Hughes never wavered in these views, even after Lincoln promulgated the Emancipation Proclamation. His critics often leveled the charge that Hughes supported slavery, a charge that was more than well documented in its untruth. Hughes in fact believed that slaves were entitled to just and decent treatment, to decent food, housing, medical care and access to religious practice. He most certainly did not believe in immediate manumission, as he believed that such a move would be injurious to the otherwise unprepared slave population. The more practical reality was that his own Irish community subsisted on the very lowest rung of American economic society and would have had to directly compete against freed slaves for the scratchings of the bottom of the economic pit. Hughes would not have been persuaded by any argument in support of improving the lot of African slaves over his own people. In this respect, Hughes acted from intellectual honesty. To Hughes, the abolitionist position with respect to the slaves represented utter, moral dishonesty. While agitating for the freeing of slaves, abolitionist opinion would have never deemed blacks the equal of whites in terms of their status after freedom was granted. Many abolitionists harbored hardly veiled nativist sentiments, and the stunning inconsistency with respect to Irish Catholic immigrants struck Hughes as both hypocritical as well as unchristian. Hughes most clearly expressed this view of abolitionists and abolitionism in a letter to Secretary of War Simon Cameron. In the correspondence, Hughes made it clear that any Northern war effort solely on behalf of slaves would have a chilling effect on the support to be expected from his own people: "There is being insinuated in this part of the country an idea to the effect that the purpose of this war is the abolition of slavery in the South. If that idea should prevail among a certain class (immigrant poor), by implication the Irish, it would make recruiting slack indeed. The Catholics, as far as I know, whether of native or foreign birth, are willing to fight to the death for support of the Constitution, the Government, and the laws of the country, but it should be understood that, with or without their knowing it, they are to fight for the abolition of slavery, then indeed, they will turn away in distrust from the discharge of what would otherwise be patriotic duty."[8]

II

The Roman Catholic population of the United States tripled in the years between 1860 and the end of the century. Numbering some 7,000,000 persons, the Catholic Church had emerged as the largest religious denomination in the country, with Irish representation in the majority. The seminal work of John Hughes in building up the New York Diocese, crown jewel of the American Catholic Church, had been substantial in the years between 1842 and 1863. In comparison, nothing approximating the growth of the Hughes tenure would be replicated until the reign of Francis Cardinal Spellman (1939-1967), whose aggressive program of church and parish building would be contributory in earning him the appellation, "American Pope."[9] In the middle decades of the nineteenth century, anti-Catholic and anti-Irish reaction had been an urban centered affair. By the beginning of the twentieth century, the focal point of nativist activity had shifted away from urban areas into the remote rural areas of places like Indiana, Michigan and Nebraska. Even the great cross burnings carried out by members of the Ku Klux Klan were generally carried out in places where Roman Catholic populations were sparse. The strident anti-Catholic tone of earlier times however had already set the pattern. John Hughes, in responding to the bigotry against his people, forced the Catholic Church to remove itself from any effort to accommodate American institutions and sought to establish a separatist structure of Catholic schools, hospitals, orphanages and even financial institutions. In New York, where government was rooted in a completely Protestant culture, it did not and would not meet the needs of an expanding Irish Catholic community. The Irish, aided and encouraged by Hughes, did it themselves. In this regard, one of the great contributions of Hughes was his establishment of a Catholic Church in New York that could neither be ignored nor taken for granted. The institutional Catholic Church had finally come of age.

The Hughes legacy was to endure bitter criticism for what his detractors would describe as forcing his people into a narrow, limited and separate path, a path they claimed would work against the Catholic Church rather than for it. Hughes, by necessity, in order to defend his Church and people, inaugurated a completely self-contained Catholic structure. While he preached Americanism and assimilation, there was no getting away from the reality of a Catholic Church whose institutions operated outside of the realm of the American body politic. The only models of growth and survival were to be found in the Irish Church, and that model was an intensely conservative one. The Church's social apostolate was to follow the same trend as did the pattern of politics, once the Irish assumed control of the levers of government through the Democratic Party machine. As Hughes saw it, one of the primary purposes of the Church was the preservation of the old order, an order that had been robbed from the people by the English oppressor. In short, so long as Roman Catholicism remained immigrant oriented, it was to remain a strongly conservative body. The insular walls that Hughes constructed around his Church had implications not only in New York but for the rest of the country as well. This construct was to form the basis of bitter, contentious battles in the last quarter of the nineteenth century amongst the American Catholic hierarchy. Within fifteen years of Hughes's death, the Catholic Church in America had grown so numerous and powerful that it was forced to take a critical look at its position within American society. The pressing question was whether or not the Church should make an attempt to more closely assimilate itself into American society or remain on the solo path that had been laid down by Hughes? Driving this question would be issues connected to labor unions, charitable outreach, ethnic assimilation and even the parochial school system itself. The emerging and often bitter debate would rage between the Americanist or "assimilationist" school of American Catholicism and the Conservative school, largely adherents of the Hughes strain of thought. Not for another century, in the bitter disputes following the deliberations of the Second Vatican Council, would the vitriol between members of the American hierarchy be greater. In addition, that so prominent a member of the Catholic Church as

Hughes should have been denied a Cardinal's red hat speaks to the more complex behind the scenes realities with respect to the position of the American Catholic Church in the second half of the nineteenth Century. While the impact of Hughes in places like New York no doubt laid the foundation for the strong and sustained growth of Roman Catholicism, certain realities could not be ignored. While Hughes indeed provided leadership from the trenches in the fight to establish the right of Catholicism to exist, the path to promotion in the Church lay in the bureaucratic rather than pastoral aspects of clerical life. A Roman education and the patronage of powerful Roman insiders provided the path to real power. Hughes had made the landing, secured the beachhead and managed to get the troops ashore. By virtue of his temperament and tactics, he kept his people intact long enough to withstand the punishment of enemy fire, enough so to find the weak spots in the enemy's defenses and exploit the breach. To others however and not Hughes would come the great breakout and ultimate victory – accommodation and acceptance of Roman Catholicism as the de facto preeminent religious group of the United States.[10]

In line with the spiritual struggles waged by Hughes, another great achievement while fighting for his people in the trenches fell within the realm of the temporal. The early Irish famine community in New York, poor as it was, still determined that others left behind in Ireland would need financial help to ameliorate the devastating effects of the potato blight. Hughes recognized the need for the establishment of a financial institution geared primarily to the special needs of Irish immigrants. Working in concert with Irish bankers and merchants, especially his countryman, Eugene O'Kelly, the Emigrant Savings Bank was established at 51 Chambers Street in lower Manhattan, opening its doors for business on the morning of September 30th, 1852. O'Kelly was typical of the hard headed men of means Hughes early surrounded himself with. Born in County Tyrone, he arrived in the United States at age twenty-two. Starting out as a clerk in a dry goods store, O'Kelly soon married the owner's sister and then proceeded to open up dry goods stores in places from Kentucky to San Francisco. As part of small cadre of trusted advisors, O'Kelly was intimately involved in formulation of the plans that resulted in the Emigrant Bank. He went to successfully establish banking houses in San Francisco and New York. Widowed, O'Kelly took a niece of John Hughes in marriage. Known for his sound financial advice, prudence and reserved nature, O'Kelly would provide financial guidance not only to Hughes, but to his successor, John McCloskey. O'Kelly's long-time friend and business partner was Dublin born Henry Hoguet, who would serve as president of the Emigrant for many years. The Emigrant Bank was no ordinary financial institution, for its purpose was twofold: 1.) Hughes determined to establish among his people the habit of thrift and savings. By powerful example, Hughes led the way by opening his own account and encouraging both Catholic priests to establish individual accounts as well as pastors to establish parish accounts with the bank as well. 2.) The bank facilitated the remittance of monies set aside by the immigrants to send home to help their struggling families. This was a first, as it specifically catered to the needs of the Irish. The overwhelming support of the Catholic clergy reinforced the idea that this was "our bank." As a result, remittances grew exponentially and by 1856, the bank could boast over 11,000 accounts and $1,300,000.00 in deposits. Once established, the bank, just as the other charitable, religious and social organizations, contributed to the ever strengthening fabric of Irish-American life. Hughes was cementing the blocks of a once broken wall back together.[11]

III

The demographics of New York City had changed since the arrival of John J. Hughes in 1838. It had grown considerably as not only a metropolis, but as a sprawling Catholic center, home to approximately 800,000 residents, roughly half of whom were foreign born and most of them Irish. Even though Irish Catholics had enlisted with enthusiasm to fight for the Union, widespread poverty, social ostracism and blatant bigotry was still widely prevalent. Advances had been made, but the summer of 1863 was to mark the overflow of long simmering frustrations within the Irish community, frustrations that were to lead to an unprecedented outbreak of violence. In one of the greatest acts of disloyalty ever displayed, the New York City Draft Riot would practically erase the years of effort to show the Irish as good and loyal Americans. While Hughes could not be personally held responsible for the actions of some, it would not be remembered as one his finest hours.

The draft had been instituted to continue a war effort that had been largely carried on by volunteer enlistments with fixed periods of service. At the end of the enlistment period, some men could and did throw away their arms because their service had terminated. As the Civil War progressed and both the Union and Confederate armies perfected the systematic slaughter that resulted in tens of thousands of casualties during a single battle, the need for bodies to feed the insatiable death machine greatly increased. The Lincoln Administration imposed the draft to insure keeping the flow of manpower continuous. All able bodied men were to register; however, there was one inequitable flaw in the system. A man was able to provide a substitute for service or buy his way out for the sum of $300.00. As this amount represented more money than the average workingman earned in a year, it was obvious where the brunt of the fighting would fall in places like New York. The war had seemingly become a wealthy man's conflict to be fought by his economic inferiors. The Civil War wore heavily on Hughes, who in failing health, was still bridling under the harshness of the attacks against him personally for having participated in the special diplomatic mission for Abraham Lincoln to Europe. Hughes knew his Irish people, and had frequently warned Secretary Seward and others of the ill effect of presenting the Union war effort as an attempt to end slavery. More and more free blacks were making their way to the North, where they challenged the Irish in the race for even the most menial of jobs, in some instances, being preferred over the detested Catholic foreigner. Lincoln's forced military draft also seeped into the brewing cauldron of discontent, as street corner agitators, especially in the poorer and working class neighborhoods of New York utilized the opportunity to denounce the dictatorial Lincoln as the Roman tyrant Caligula who wrote to his mother, "I have power in all things, and over all persons."[12]

Ominous signs of trouble continued to manifest themselves. In the wake of the carnage at Gettysburg, where Union and Confederate casualties totaled almost 50,000 in three days of savage fighting between July 1st and July 3rd, 1863, Democratic Governor of New York, Horatio Seymour, stirred the simmering cauldron with an Independence Day speech accusing the Lincoln Administration of further tyranny in stating "that the bloody, treasonable and revolutionary doctrine of public necessity can be proclaimed by a mob as well as a government."[13]

Now, the simmering pot started to boil. Throughout the week, newspapers started to print the names of those who had fallen in battle. Among the names of the dead were considerable numbers of men with Irish surnames. In a bigoted assault against the Irish, Horace Greeley published an open letter to Archbishop Hughes in which he blamed the Irish for helping to not only bring about the Civil war, but for the refusal of Catholic priests to preach abolition of Negroes. "Your people for years have been and today are foremost in the degredation and abuse of the persecuted race."[14]

The drawing of the names for the draft began peacefully enough on Sunday, July 11th. All throughout the hot and humid enclaves of impoverished Irish areas, malcontents and Democratic ward politicians were spreading rumors about the heavy-handed, oppressive and unconstitutional tactics of Lincoln. As workingmen headed to their local taverns to drink, Sunday being their only day of recreation, street corner orators played more and more to the pent-up anger finding release with the emptying of each barrel of beer. Monday dawned, hot, humid and steamy, an omen of what was to shortly become the worst outbreak of racial violence and property destruction ever witnessed in New York up until that time. At the draft offices located at Forty-Sixth Street and Third Avenue, a large crowd had gathered and commenced an attack on the buildings and occupants shortly before noon. Many factory workers and street car employees joined in the mayhem. The buildings were soon filled with the crackling sound of tall flames, as thick, gray smoke engulfed the entire area. A detachment of the army provost guard arrived on the scene along with a small detail of police, but to no avail. They were quickly overcome by the drink inflamed mob. Recording the events in his diary, George Templeton Strong wrote "Every brute in the drove was pure Celtic, hod carrier or loafer."[15]

The situation at the draft offices quickly spread, as the city exploded in bloody violence. As the day wore on, thousands of Irish immigrants participated in burning, looting and battling of the undersized police force. The Irish mob showed particular malice toward blacks, and many were literally hunted down in the streets to be beaten, shot or hung from trees or lamp posts. After four days of intensive street fighting, battle hardened troops from the Army of the Potomac, rushed from the battlefield at Gettysburg, were finally able to restore order.

The Hughes response or lack thereof to the situation in the street during the riot has been the source of tremendous criticism for generations. Could Hughes have more effectively utilized the authority of his office to return calm and order? Did in fact his aggressive posture and past positions make the events a fatal inevitability? The matter deserves closer scrutiny. When it was evident that events had grown monstrously out of control, Governor Seymour as well as Horace Greeley sharply reversed their own inflammatory rhetoric and appealed to Hughes to use his powerful position to put an end to the destructive forces overtaking the city, with Greeley reminding his *Tribune* readership how Hughes had in fact been one of the first people to call for a draft. Hughes did not however take the bait, and excoriated what he believed to be the hypocrisy of Greeley. Hughes argued how the *Tribune* had consistently defended the right of rebels to overthrow the temporal power of the Pope. What was different about New York? Hughes then issued this statement to those who were rioting: "In spite of Mr. Greeley's assault upon the Irish, in the present disturbed condition of the city, I will appeal not only to them, but to all persons who love God and revere the Holy Catholic religion, which they profess, to respect also the laws of man and the peace of society, to retire to their homes with as little delay as possible, and disconnect themselves from the seemingly deliberate intention to disturb the peace and social rights of the citizens of New York."[16]

There is no question that the Catholic priests of the Archdiocese were steadfast among the rioters trying to exert peaceful influence, to stop the unbridled violence against blacks and property, and to admonish the rioters to disengage from such senseless and anti-Catholic behavior. Here again, Greeley, hypocritically appealed to Hughes to ride on horseback amongst "his people" for the purpose of maximizing the full effect of his influence to stop the chaos. Here again, Hughes's acidic reaction was that "Mr. Greeley treats me as if I were a head constable. It is for the civil authorities to take care of all the people. If they cannot do this they are incompetent to take care of themselves or protect us, and they might as well give us public notice of the fact and then go to bed."[17] What especially angered Hughes over the arrogance of Greeley's statement was the reference to the rioters as being "his people." While it was undeniably true that many of the rioters were in fact Irish and Catholic, there were many more Catholics under the pastoral care of John Hughes who were neither participants nor supporters of the violence taking place. Hughes's "people" were those who loved God, the Catholic Church and who had also given their lives in battle in defense of the country and preservation of the Union. The biting irony of it all was that throughout the period of the worst excesses in terms of Catholic Church burnings and anti-Catholic activity, the civil authorities did precious little to stem or stop the tide of attacks against the Catholic Church. Hughes was saying the same thing to Horace Greeley that he had said to New York Mayor Robert Hunter Morris in the 1840s... It is the role and the proper place of the government and civil authority to protect everyone! Still, the outbreak was a heart breaking experience for Hughes. It was heart breaking because of the intensive feeling of betrayal. It was the sudden and disappointing realization that perhaps nativists had been right about the

Irish all along. Was it true that the Irish were beyond being molded into the upstanding Republican minded citizens envisioned by Anglo-Saxon, Protestant Americans? Perhaps there was another inescapable dimension for which even Hughes, in spite of his past aggressive posturing, could not accept culpability for, namely, that America's deeply ingrained prejudice against those who were different was both systemic as well as systematic. Just as the Blackman would make the torment of his oppression known in the smoldering cities of 1960s America, the Irish were teaching their social superiors in the 1860s a lesson about where systems of pervasive bigotry and discrimination ultimately lead. The determination of one branch of society to thwart and impede the successful assimilation of those seeking to reap the benefits of liberty and a better life materially because they are different is the legacy of American nativism. Hughes circulated a letter, forwarded to all the newspapers asking that all Catholic rioters immediately cease and desist from mob action or unchristian practices. He followed by delivering a notice that he would deliver an address from his Madison Avenue residence on July 16th. Hughes was in ill health, and the actual address was delayed a day. Though enfeebled with rheumatism, Hughes nonetheless delivered a forceful and resolute address to approximately 5,000 persons from the steps of his home. While Hughes had given an impressive performance, and his followers quietly dispersed and went home to their shacks and shanties, arrival of the army had already rendered the point moot. Firmly under control of a force numbering several thousand, New York's streets were finally quiet and being patrolled by a combined Union cavalry and infantry force. Seated before the throng assembled in front of his residence, the aging Hughes told the crowd that "Everyman has a right to defend his home or his shanty at the risk of life. The cause, however, must be just. It must not be aggressive or offensive. Do you want my advice? Well, I have been hurt by the report that you were rioters. You cannot imagine that I could hear these things without being grievously pained. Is there not some way by which you can stop these proceedings and support the laws, none of which have been enacted against you as Irishmen or

Catholics. You have suffered already. No government can save itself unless it protects its citizens. Military force will be let loose upon you. The innocent will be shot down and the guilty will be likely to escape."[18]

It will always be open to question as to why Hughes was not more forceful in quickly acting to quell the disorder. Cynics have speculated that it was payback for decades of Protestant nativist indifference to the plight of violence against Catholic persons and property. Others have speculated that Hughes was physically too infirm by this point in his career to have launched and followed-up with the kind of vigorous effort that had characterized many of his past actions. A more accurate explanation maybe that Hughes, on one level, was more sympathetic to the rioters than the needs of the New York Protestant power establishment. He most certainly could have exercised tremendous influence by personally directing the rioters to cease and desist as he did in the end. Whether he would have been completely heeded by the people is open to question? The train of grievances of Irish Catholics against the elitist cast and their surrogates had long surpassed the level of passive acceptance. One thing is categorically clear: Hughes believed that just as past city governments had failed to protect "all of the people" in times of civil strife, i.e., nativist burnings of Catholic churches, so too were they now equally incapable of doing any better. "All" of his people, much to Hughes's chagrin, had not participated in this outbreak of lawlessness, and therefore, the city had as much of an obligation, if not more, to protect them as well. Hughes was a churchman and not representative of city government; the city government had clearly failed in its obligation to protect all of its citizens. In attempting to have Hughes quell the mob, the clear reference that all of "his" people were exclusively the lawbreakers did not sit well with the aging prelate, who know doubt saw by implication the same brand of bigotry that had characterized all of his past involvement with the New York nativist power structure. The Draft Riot of 1863 was not, as other detractors of Hughes have suggested, a grand conspiracy or Catholic insurrectionist plot for the purpose of laying the groundwork for invasion of a Papal army. Irish Catholics were still in the cellar of American society, unfairly asked to shed their blood for a country still not prepared to allow them to fully share in the fruit of its benefits. It was also a reflection of a greater tension within the Irish community itself, as the "haves" battled the "have-nots." Proof of this division could be seen in the ferocity with which the rioters battled their own fellow immigrants serving as police officers, many of whom were Irish-born men. No police force ever demonstrated braver or more resolute action in the face of danger, or showed more courage and devotion to duty throughout the four days of rioting.

IV

In the end, the old lion quietly retired more and more from the public gaze, declining to enter into the public arena. John Hughes may not have been the most learned theologian or most spellbinding preacher. In spite of his shortcomings and combative disposition, there was not a single member within the American Catholic hierarchy who was as influential or who possessed a greater reputation and standing in the minds of the general public, Catholic or Protestant. He was one of those clerics who, from his earliest years, had a rare combination of the important elements of greatness. He was a man who was able to create the impression that he was in possession of greater powers than in fact he had. In addition, whatever his flaws and deficiencies, he totally believed in his own powers and abilities. His confidence was not born of avarice or vanity, rather it grew from his unyielding belief in whatever cause he assumed. While it is true that he was a man of ambition, it was not an ambition directed toward personal gain or the attainment of worldly comfort. He directed every fiber of his being toward the accomplishment of advancing his Roman Catholic Church and his flock. He was also a fearless man in that he could never accept the notion of failure, even when failure seemed imminent. As a public man, he demonstrated an acute intelligence with respect to the great political issues of the day, frequently consulted by American presidents and prominent legislative figures. This was true on the international stage as well, where Hughes had the respect and confidence of heads of state and the Pope himself. He was admired because he never wavered in taking on an antagonist or forcefully explaining the positions of his Catholic Faith and Church.

Archbishop Bedini was once asked a priest as to why it was that Hughes enjoyed greater notoriety and popular attention more than any other prelate in the United States. The priest's answer to Bedini's question was "I think that it is because he is always game."[19]

Perhaps, most significantly, there was never any charge of impurity with respect to his personal character. No matter how much people may have questioned his denial of political involvement, highhandedness with trustees and even his own priests, nobody, not even his most ferocious opponents, could ever question the impeccable nature of his personal morality and integrity as a human being. Hughes died in his Madison Avenue residence on Thirty-sixth Street at 7:00 P.M. on the evening of January 3rd, 1864. In attendance with Hughes at the time of his death were his two sisters, Bishop Loughlin of Brooklyn, Father Starrs and Father McNeirny. The immediate cause of death was determined to have been the result of Bright's Disease of the Kidneys.[20] In death, Hughes loomed large and controversial, just as he had in life. George Templeton Strong may have well reflected the strong feelings of Hughes's lifelong enemies: "Archbishop Hughes is dead. Pity he survived last June and committed the imbecility of address to rioters last July. That speech blotted and spoiled a record which the Vatican must have held respectable, and against which protestants had nothing to say, except of course, "Babylon, Scarlet Women and anti-Christ,"[21]

At the conclusion of the Hughes funeral oration, delivered by Archbishop John McCloskey, the man who succeeded Hughes as well as being named America's first member of the College of Cardinals, we have these poignant remarks that were to become a mediation on the life and times of the Lion of American Catholicism, a Lion whose roar paved the way for the making of America's Kingdom of God: "If there was ever a man who, in the whole history and character of his life, impressed upon us the sense and the conviction that he had been raised up by God, was chosen as His instrument to do an appointed work, and was strengthened by His grace and supported by His wisdom for the accomplishment of the work for which he had been chosen and appointed, the man was Archbishop Hughes. He was from the beginning until the end, clearly and plainly an instrument in the hands of God."[22]

Chapter Notes

Chapter 1

Uneasy Relationship in the Land of Liberty

1. Horvat, Marian T., Ph.D., *Let None Dare Call it Liberty: The Catholic Church in Colonial America:* [http://www. traditioninaction.org/History/B 001 Colonies.html]: paragraph 3: Retrieved [10/17/2016].
2. A. C. Partridge, *English Biblical Translation,* (London, Andre Deutsch: 1973), pp. 38-39.
3. Horvat, Marian T., PhD., paragraph 18.
4. Ibid, paragraph 20.
5. Ibid, paragraph 21.
6. Ibid, paragraph 23.
7. Ibid, paragraph 25.
8. Ibid, paragraph 24.
9. Keiley, Jarvis, *The Catholic Encyclopedia.* Vol 6. New York: Robert Appleton Company. Retrieved April 7th, 2016 from New Advent: http://www.newadvent.org. cathen/06460a.htm.
10. John Tracy Ellis, *Catholics in Colonial America,* (Baltimore: 1965), pp. 315-359.
11. Ibid, p.363.
12. Sally Schwartz, *"A Mixed Multitude." The Struggle for Toleration in Colonial Pennsylvania,* (New York and London: 1987), pp. 15-16.
13. Daniel Walker Howe, *What Hath God Wrought: The Transformation of America, 1815-1848* (New York: Oxford University Press), p. 197.

14. Ibid, p. 197.
15. Ibid, p. 198.
16. Ibid, pp.198-199.
17. Brooks Mather Kelley, *Yale: A History*, (Yale University Press: 1974) p. 130.
18. Daniel Walker Howe, pp. 285-288.
19. Ibid, p. 1.
20. Quoted in Richard Shaw, *Dagger John: The Unquiet Life and Times of Archbishop John Hughes of New York*, (New York: Paulist Press, 1977), p. 93.
21. Charles R. Morris, *American Catholic: The Saints and Sinners Who Built America's Most Powerful Church*, (Times Books: 1997), pp. 54-55.
22. Ibid, pp. 55-59.
23. Ibid, quoted on p. 59.
24. George Adams Boyd, *Elias Boudinot, Patriot and Statesman, 1740-1821*, (London: Greenwood Press, 1952), p. 352.
25. Quoted in Ray Allen Billington, *The Protestant Crusade 1800-1860: A Study of the Origins of American Nativism*, (New York: Quadrangle Books, 1964), p. 143.
26. Quoted in Richard Shaw, p. 142.
27. John T. McGreevy, *Catholicism and American Freedom*, (New York and London: W.W. Norton & Co., 2003), pp.7-8.
28. Ibid, p. 8.
29. Ibid, pp. 9-10.
30. Ibid, p. 11.
31. Ibid, p. 10.
32. August Meier and Elliot Rudnick, *From Plantation to Ghetto*, Third Edition, (Toronto: McGraw-Hill Ryerson Ltd., 1976) pp. 57-63.
33. Ibid, p. 50.
34. Ibid, pp. 51-54.
35. Ibid, p. 54.
36. **In Supremo Apostolatus** – A Papal Bull issued by Pope Gregory XVI addressing the issue of slavery. Issued on December 3rd, 1839, the Bull denounced both the slave trade and its continuance. Imprecise language lent itself to much debate and controversy over the decades, with many American Catholic Church leaders choosing to

interpret the document in relation to American state laws, where slavery was to be left unmolested in the places it already existed.

37. Kenneth J. Zanca, ed., *American Catholics and Slavery: 1789-1866* (New York: University Press of America, 1994), p. 36.

Chapter 2

An Unlikely Descendant of the Apostles

1. John Hassard, *Life of the Most Reverend John Hughes, First Archbishop of New York,* (New York: Cosimo Classics, 2008), pp. 21-27.
2. Richard Shaw, pp. 21-22.
3. Quoted in Hassard, p. 42.
4. Ibid, p.30.
5. Ibid, p. 24-25.
6. G.A. Hayes McCoy, *"The Tudor Conquest, 1534-1603": The Course of Irish History,* ed., T.W. Moody and F.X. Martin, (Cork, Ireland: Mercier Press, 1967), p. 183.
7. Ibid, p. 218.
8. Ibid, p. 218.
9. Hassard, p. 13.
10. **Orangemen** – The network of Protestant organizations devoted to the humiliation and physical confrontation with Roman Catholics.
11. **Ribbonmen** – The network of Catholic organizations dedicated to physical confrontations with Protestants.
12. Extract from "Parochial Records," Diocese of Clogher, by the Reverend J.E. McKenna, P.P., printed in the Fermanagh Herald Office, Enniskillen, 1920.
13. Hassard, pp. 15-17.
14. Quoted in Richard Shaw, p. 15.
15. Quoted in Henry Athanasius Brann, *Most Reverend John Hughes, First Archbishop of New York,* (New York: Dodd, Mead and Company, 1892), p. 28.
16. Ibid, p. 30.
17. Hughes to Bruté, [No Date], quoted in Hassard, p. 35.

18. Ibid, quoted on p. 23.
19. Henry Athanasius Brann, pp. 29-31.
20. Hurley to Hughes, November, 1825, quoted in Hassard, p. 47.
21. Ibid, p. 47.
22. Ibid, pp. 49-50.
23. Ibid, pp. 41-42.
24. Quoted in Richard Shaw, p. 41.

Chapter 3

Lessons in the Rough and Tumble of Diocesan Life

1. Richard Shaw, pp. 27-28.
2. Henry Athanasius Brann, p. 34.
3. Hassard, p. 54.
4. Ibid, quoted on p. 50.
5. Ibid, Egan to Hughes, February 5th, 1827, quoted on pp. 55-56.
6. Quoted in Richard Shaw, p. 44.
7. **Congregation of the Propaganda** – *The Sacred Congregation of the Propaganda Fide,* is the department of the pontifical administration charged with the spread of Catholicism and with the regulation of ecclesiastical affairs in non-Catholic countries.
8. Richard Shaw, pp. 45-46.
9. Quoted in Henry Athanasius Brann, p. 36.
10. Richard Shaw, pp. 48-49.
11. Hughes to Bruté, May 14th, 1828, quoted in Hassard, p. 68.
12. Quoted in Richard Shaw, p. 51.
13. Ibid, p. 53.
14. G. A. Hayes-McCoy, *The Tudor Conquest*, p. 218.
15. **On the Emancipation of Irish Catholics, Preached in the Church of St. Augustine, Philadelphia, May 31st, 1829**, quoted in Lawrence Kehoe, ed., *Complete Works of the Most Reverend John Hughes, D.D., Archbishop of New York, Comprising His Sermons, Letters, Lectures,*

Etc., Volume 1, (New York: Lawrence Kehoe, 7 Beekman Street, 1866), p. 31.

16. Quoted in Richard Shaw, p. 58.
17. Ibid, p. 58.
18. Quoted in Hassard, p. 93.
19. **"mitre and crozier"** – A **mitre** is the official head dress of a Roman Catholic bishop and the **crozier** is his staff.
20. Hughes to his sister, Ellen Hughes, September 17th, 1829, quoted in Hassard, p. 95.
21. Ibid, p. 100.
22. Excerpt from *The Protestant,* March 13th, 1830, quoted in Hassard, p. 106.
23. Ibid, p. 107. Excerpt from a letter of John Hughes entitled **"To the Ministers of The Gospel, Who Have recommended *The Protestant* to the patronage of a Christian public,"** July, 1830.
24. Thomas F. Meehan, *The Catholic Historical Review,* Vol. 4, No. 4, (January, 1919), p. 414.
25. Hughes to Purcell, September 27th, 1830, quoted in Hassard, p. 109.

Chapter 4

Catholicism Comes Out of the Shadows

1. Richard Shaw, pp. 82-85.
2. Ibid, quoted on p. 85.
3. Ibid, quoted on p. 85.
4. Ibid, quoted on p. 86.
5. Walter Lynwood Fleming, *The South in the Building of a Nation,* Biography, Volume 11, ed., (Richmond: The Southern Historical Publication Society, 1919), p. 117.
6. Hughes to Breckinridge, October 3rd, 1831, quoted in *Controversy Between the Reverend John Hughes of the Roman Catholic Church and the Reverend John Breckinridge of the Presbyterian Church, Relative to the Existing Difference between the Roman Catholic and Presbyterian Religions,* originally published in the Presbyterian,

Philadelphia: John Whiteman, 22 South Fourth Street, 1833.

7. Ibid, Breckinridge to Hughes, October 13th, 1832, preface.
8. Ibid, quoted in preface.
9. Ibid, Hughes to Breckinridge, January 21st, 1833, quoted on p. 2.
10. Ibid, quoted on p. 3.
11. Ibid, quoted on p. 5.
12. Ibid, Breckinridge to Hughes, February 2nd, 1833, quoted on p. 15.
13. Ibid, quoted on p. 15.
14. Ibid, Hughes to Breckinridge, February 14th, 1833, quoted on p. 20.
15. Ibid, quoted on p. 23.
16. Ibid, Breckinridge to Hughes, February 18th, 1833, quoted on p. 29.
17. Ibid, quoted on p. 29.
18. Richard Shaw, p. 89.
19. Quoted in *Controversy Between*, Breckinridge to Hughes, March 21st, 1833, p. 58.
20. Ibid, Hughes to Breckinridge, March 21st, 1833, quoted on p. 70.
21. Hughes to Bruté, April 5th, 1833, quoted in Hassard, p. 142.
22. Quoted in *Controversy Between*, Hughes to Bruté, May 22, 1833, p. 135.
23. Ibid, p. 135.
24. Ibid, Breckinridge to Hughes, May 30th, 1833, p. 147.
25. Ibid, p. 147.
26. Ibid, Hughes to Breckinridge, June 20th, 1833, quoted on p. 170.
27. Quoted in Hassard, p. 143.
28. Ibid, Hughes to Bruté, March 8th, 1833, quoted on p. 140.
29. Ibid, quoted on p. 144.
30. Ibid, quoted on p. 147.
31. Ibid, p. 147.
32. Ibid, p. 154.

33. Ibid, Breckinridge to Hughes, January 21st, 1835, quoted on p. 155.
34. Ibid, p. 155.
35. *A Discussion of the Question is the Roman Catholic Religion in any or all its Principles and Doctrines, Inimical to Civil or Religious Liberty? And of the Question, is the Presbyterian Religion in any or all its Principles or Doctrines Inimical to Civil or Religious Liberty? By the Reverend John Hughes of the Roman Catholic Church and the Reverend John Breckinridge of the Presbyterian Church*, (Philadelphia: Carey, Lea and Blanchard, 1836), Definitions and Conditions.
36. Ibid, p. 5.
37. Ibid, p. 44.
38. Ibid, p. 59.
39. Ibid, p. 75.
40. Ibid, p. 76.
41. Hassard, p. 159.
42. Henry Athanasius Brann, p. 54.
43. Hassard p. 160.
44. Ibid, p. 160.
45. Richard Shaw, p. 99.
46. Henry Athanasius Brann, p. 55.
47. Hassard, pp. 179-180.
48. Richard Shaw, p. 17.

Chapter 5

The Fight for Catholic Education

1. Extract from the Funeral Oration of Archbishop John McCloskey, January 7th, 1864, quoted in Hughes, Complete Works, Vol. 1, pp. 18-19.
2. Richard Shaw, p. 117.
3. Ibid, p. 117.
4. Ibid, quoted on p. 119.
5. Ibid, quoted on p. 121.

6. Shelley, Thomas J., *"Archbishop John Hughes and the Church in New York,"* Catholic New York, July 6th, 2000. http://cnv.org/archive/ft/ft070600.htm.
7. Hughes to Frenaye, January 3rd, 1838, quoted in Hassard, p. 183.
8. Henry Athanasius Brann, pp. 60-62.
9. Hassard, p. 213.
10. Hughes to Varela, June 1st, 1840, quoted in Hassard, p. 220.
11. Quoted in Ray Allen Billington, p. 143.
12. David O'Brien, *Public Catholicism*, (Chicago: McMillan Publishing Company, 1996), p. 44.
13. **Whore of Babylon** – In the lexicon of anti-Catholic bigotry, the "Whore of Babylon" was always understood to be the Pope and Catholic Church. The expression comes from the Book of Revelation, the last book of the Old Testament.
14. David O'Brien, p. 45.
15. Documents of the Assembly of the State of New York, 63rd Session, 1840, Document Number 2, pp. 5-6.
16. Hughes, Complete Works, Vol. 1, p. 102.
17. Ibid, quoted on p. 44.
18. Ibid, p. 41.
19. Ibid, quoted on p. 50.
20. Ibid, quoted on p. 79.
21. Ibid, quoted on p. 79.
22. Ibid, quoted on p. 79.
23. Ibid, quoted on p. 126.
24. Ibid, quoted on p. 132.
25. Ibid, quoted on p. 135.
26. Ibid, quoted on p. 143.
27. Quoted in Hassard, p. 243.
28. Quoted in Hughes, Complete Works, Vol. 1, p. 272.
29. Quoted in Hassard, p. 245.
30. Ibid, p. 245.
31. **Locofocos** – The name of the workingman's wing of the Democratic Party in New York City, who took their name from a meeting in Tammany Hall on October 25th, 1835. The party regulars had nominated their own slate of candidates for the upcoming municipal

elections and declared the meeting adjourned. When disaffected workers tried to contest the outcome and prolong the meeting, the gas lights were turned out. The dissenters had come prepared however with the newest sulfur friction matches called "locofocos" or "lucifers."

32. Don Seitz, *The James Gordan Bennetts, Father and Son, Proprietors of New York,* (New York: Houghton-Mifflin, 1959), p. 107.

33. Quoted in Alan Nevins and Milton Halsey Thomas, ed., *The Diary of George Templeton Strong: Young Man in New York, 1835-1849,* (New York: The McMillan Company, 1952), pp. 177-178.

Chapter 6

Building and Defending an Immigrant Church

1. E.R.R. Green, *The Great Famine, 1845-1850, "The Course of Irish History,"* ed., W.W. Moody and F.X. Martin, (Cork, Ireland: Mercier Press, 1967), p. 267.

2. **Partible Inheritance** – The practice of dividing land among all sons.

3. Helen Litton, *The Irish Famine, An Illustrated History,* (Dublin: Wolfhound Press, 1994), p. 15.

4. E.R.R. Green, p. 274.

5. Oscar Handlin, *The Uprooted,* (Little, Brown and Company, 1951), p. 125.

6. Helen Litton, p. 108.

7. David Fitzpatrick, *"Flight from Famine:" The Great Irish Famine,* ed., Cathal Portier, (Dublin: Mercier Press, 1995), p. 179.

8. Leo Hershkowitz, *"The Irish and the Emerging City, Settlement to 1844,"* Ronald H. Baylor and Timothy Meagher, *The New York Irish,* ed., (Baltimore: John Hopkins University Press, 1996), p. 20.

9. Quoted in Hassard, p. 303.

10. Richard Shaw, p. 209.

11. Quoted in Hassard, p. 312.

12. David Gibson, *"St. Brigid's Parish, A Pilgrim Church from an Immigrant People,"* Catholics in New York Society, Culture and Politics, 1808-1946, ed., Terry Golway, (New York: Fordham University Press, 2008), pp. 55-57.
13. New York Daily Tribune, November 6th, 1843.
14. David M. Potter, *The Impending Crisis, 1848-1861*: Completed and Edited by Don E. Fehrenbacher, (New York: Harper Row Publishers, Inc., 1976), pp. 244-246.
15. Quoted in Charles R. Morris, p. 9.
16. Nathan Glazer and Daniel P. Moynihan, *Beyond the Melting Pot: The Negroes, Puerto Ricans, Jews, Italians and Irish of New York City*, (Cambridge, Mass.: MIT Press, 1970), p. 237.
17. Quoted in Richard Shaw, p. 223.
18. Ibid, p. 222.
19. Ibid, quoted on p. 225.
20. Henry Athanasius Brann, p. 96.
21. Ibid, quoted on p. 90.
22. Hassard, p. 280.
23. Richard Shaw, p. 202.
24. Catholics in New York Society, Culture and Politics, 1808-1846, p. 83.

Chapter 7

America's Most Esteemed Catholic Churchman

1. Hassard, p. 288.
2. Melba Porter Hay, *The Papers of Henry Clay: Candidate, Compromiser, Elder Statesman*, Volume 10, ed., (Lexington, Kentucky: The University Press of Kentucky, 1991), p. 140.
3. Hassard, p. 288.
4. Doris Kearns Goodwin, *Team of Rivals: The Political Genius of Abraham Lincoln*, (New York: Simon and Schuster, 2005), p. 73.
5. Harriet A. Weed, *Autobiography of Thurlow Weed*, ed., (Boston: Houghton, Mifflin and Company, 1884), pp. 483-484.

6. Ibid, p. 484.
7. Quoted in Hassard, p. 248.
8. Ibid, p. 249.
9. Mary E. Meline and Edward F. X. McSweeny, *The Story of the Mountain*, (Published by the Emmitsburg Chronicle, 1911).
10. Alan Nevins, ed., Polk: *The Diary of a President, 1845-1849*, (New York: Capricorn Books, 1929), pp. 97-98.
11. Church Times, June 9th, 1846.
12. New York Herald Tribune, July 2nd, 1846.
13. Sister Blanche Marie McEniry, M.A., *American Catholics in the War with Mexico*, (PhD diss., Gettysburg Times and News Publishing Company, 1937), pp. 41-42.
14. *Hughes, Complete Works*, Vol., p. 559.
15. Ibid, p. 559.
16. Ibid, p. 559.
17. Ibid, p. 561.
18. Ibid, p. 569.
19. Ibid, p. 570.
20. Ibid, p. 578.
21. Ibid, p. 578.
22. **Pallium** – A white woolen band with four purple crosses worn by Roman Catholic archbishops and primates as a symbol of their sharing in the fullness of the episcopal office with the Pope.
23. Lawrence Kehoe, ed., *Complete Works of the Most Reverend John Hughes, D.D., Archbishop of New York, Comprising His Sermons, Letters, Lectures and Speeches, Etc.*, Volume 2, (New York: Lawrence Kehoe, 7 Beekman Street, 1866), p. 36.
24. Hassard, p. 341.
25. James F. Connelly, *The Visit of Archbishop Gaetano Bedini to the United States of America: June, 1853 – February, 1854*, (Rome: Gregorian University, 1960), p. 7.
26. Ibid, p. 8.
27. Quoted in Hassard p. 357.
28. Richard Shaw, p. 276.
29. James F. Connelly, p. 8.
30. Quoted in Richard Shaw, pp. 286-287.
31. Ibid, quoted on p. 288.

32. Ibid, quoted on p. 288.
33. Ibid, p. 288.
34. Ibid, p. 288.

Chapter 8

Preserving the Union

1. David M. Potter., pp. 51-56.
2. Ibid, pp. 442-443.
3. Doris Kearns Goodwin, quoted on p. 6.
4. Ibid, pp. 247-250.
5. Ibid, pp. 293-337.
6. Ibid, pp. 263-271.
7. Ibid, quoted on p. 277.
8. Hughes, *Complete Works,* Vol. 2, p. 756.
9. James McPherson, Battle Cry of Freedom, (New York: Oxford University Press, 1988), p. 507.
10. Kenneth J. Zanca, p. 36.
11. Ibid, p. 244.
12. New York Times, April 21st, 1861.
13. Edward K. Spann, *"The Union Green, The Irish Community and the Civil War,"* The New York Irish, p. 197.
14. Ibid, p. 199.
15. Abraham Lincoln papers at the Library of Congress. Transcribed and Annotated by the Lincoln Studies Center, Knox College, Galesburg, Illinois. (Letter from Abraham Lincoln to John Hughes [Draft], October 21st, 1861.
16. Hughes, *Complete Works*, Vol. 2, p. 761.
17. Ibid, p. 762.
18. Harpers Weekly, November 23rd, 1861.
19. Rena Mazyck Andrews, *Archbishop John Hughes and the Civil War*, (PhD. Diss., University of Chicago, 1935), pp. 7-8.
20. Quoted in Hassard, pp. 490-491.
21. Ibid, p. 491.

22. Ibid, p. 486.
23. Ibid, p. 489.

Chapter 9

The Lion's Legacy

1. Jay P. Dolan, *The Immigrant Church, New York's German and Irish Catholics, 1815-1865*, (John Hopkins University Press, 1977), p. 70.
2. Ibid, p. 72.
3. Quoted in Archbishop John Hughes and the Church in New York.
4. Quoted in Charles R. Morris, p. 75.
5. *Catholic Church in New York*, Volume 1, (2 Volumes, New York and Boston, 1905), p. 78.
6. Hasia R. Diner, *"The Most Irish City in the Union:" The Era of the Great Migration, The New York Irish,* ed., Ronald H. Baylor and Timothy J. Meagher), p. 105.
7. Quoted in Henry Athanasius Brann, p. 106.
8. Ibid, p. 106.
9. John Cooney, *American Pope: The Life and Times of Francis Cardinal Spellman*, (New York: Times Publishing, 1984), Introduction.
10. Charles R. Morris, pp. 84-85.
11. Tyler Anbinder, *"Saving Grace, The Emigrant Savings Bank and its Depositors," Catholics in New York: Society, Culture and Politics*, 1808-1846, ed., Terry Golway, (New York: Fordham University Press, 2008), p. 83.
12. Quoted in Richard Shaw, p. 361.
13. Ibid, p. 361.
14. Ibid, p. 362.
15. Allan Nevins and Milton Halsey Thomas, ed., *The Diary of George Templeton Strong: The Civil War, 1860-1865,* (New York: The McMillan Company, 1952), p. 335.
16. Ibid, p. 365.
17. Ibid, p. 366.
18. William Allan Bates, Tiger in the Streets: A City in Time of Trouble, (New York, 1966), p. 147.
19. Hassard, p. 504.

20. Ibid, p. 502.
21. *The Diary of George Templeton Strong: The Civil War,* p. 390.
22. Hassard, pp. 504-505.

Index